Diet Box meals

3 Books in 1

Book 1-Intermittent Fasting

Book 2-Ketogenic Miracle

Book 3-Ketogenic Diet for Beginners

With Healthy & Low-Carb Recipes for Beginners

By: Emily Simmons

Copyright ©2019 by Emily Simmons

All rights reserved. No part of this book

May be used or reproduced in any matter

Whatsoever without permission in writing from

The author except in the case of brief quotations

Embodied in critical articles or review.

Table of Contents

Books 1:Intermittent Fasting

Chapter One: How Does Intermittent Fasting Work and What Are Its Benefits 16

Chapter Two: Some Myths Busted and Who Should Avoid Intermittent Fasting 35

Chapter Three: Methods of Intermittent Fasting 43

Chapter Four: Tips to Start off, what to Expect in the Initial Days and How to Manage Them 59

Chapter Six: Mistakes to Avoid and Other Important Information about Intermittent Fasting 87

Conclusion 97

Mistake No.11   Poor timing 149

Things to remember before following the ketogenic diet and why should you consume high fat with moderate levels of proteins? 167

Targeted Ketogenic Diet and Cyclical Ketogenic Diet169

Who should follow the ketogenic diet? 169

Benefits of the ketogenic diet171

Dangers of the ketogenic diet171

Side effects of the ketogenic diet172

Coconut Oil Fried 176

Grilled Chicken Wings with Salsa and Veg177

Eggs and Bacon180

Ground Beef & Bell Peppers-182

Low-Carb No Bun Cheeseburgers-185

Fried Chicken Breasts-188

Fake Meat Pizza-191

Cheesy Egg & Bacon-194

Spicy Shrimp & Mashed Cauliflower-197

Bacon & Brussels Sprouts-200

Easy & Quick Tomato Soup-203

Salami with Goat Cheese-206

Stuffed Deviled Eggs-209

Low Carb Chili Beef in Rich Tomato Gravy212

Keto Quick Gravy-215

Southern Spicy Chicken Salad-218

Keto Spinach Soup-221

Orange Coconut Drink-224

Salmon Spread-227

Fried Eggs With Cheddar Garlic and Cooking Grits-228

Cup Omelets-231

Tomato Scoops filled with Avocado-234

White Bean Salmon Salad-235

Chicken Lettuce Burrito-239

Shrimp Skewers and Lime Honey Dipping Sauce-243

Zucchini Wraps-247

Eggs and Kale Blessing-250

Shrimp, Avocado and Spinach Salad with Lemon Zest Dressing-253

Flour Free Cheese Crackers-256

Bok Choy and Crispy Tofu Salad-259

Cheese Broccoli Soup-264

Avocado Wrapped in Bacon-265

Salmon Baked with Herbs-269

Peppermint Bombs-273

Pistachio Almond Fat Bombs-275

Mushroom Sauce and Steak-278

Books 1:

Intermittent Fasting

A Beginner's Guidebook for Men and Women to Challenge Crash Diets and Achieve Effective Weight Loss and Fitness Naturally

By: Emily Simmons

Introduction: A Brief Prelude to Intermittent Fasting

Intermittent fasting is not a diet but merely an eating pattern. Fasting is one of the most natural forms of healing that has been in existence from time immemorial. It is not just humans but even animals that do not eat when they are sick. Resting the digestive system during times of physical stress such as an illness facilitates improved healing naturally.

You don't need to go very far to understand the connection between fasting to illness. Recall the last time you fell sick. It could be something as simple as a cold-cough or a bout of viral flu. During that time, the thought of food brought on a feeling of nausea, right? That was a sign from your body urging you to abstain from eating until your sickness was healed.

Any living being's natural instinct is to stay away from food during sickness to allow the body to begin the healing process. When the healing is completed, the appetite will return naturally. The ancient Greek physician, Hippocrates, said, "To eat when you are sick is like feeding the sickness." Plutarch, another philosopher and wise man from the ancient Greek-Roman times, said, "Instead of using medicine, rather, fast a day."

So, what is intermittent fasting? Here is a brief answer to this question. The modern world calls for eating 3-4 (sometimes 4-6 small meals too) meals a day including breakfast, lunch, a small snack with your afternoon tea and dinner. Intermittent fasting calls for reducing the number of meals from 3-4 to 1-2. Other than this, there are few restrictions on what you can eat. Before we go into the details of intermittent fasting, how it works, its various benefits, and how to implement it in your life, let us delve into its history briefly.

History of Intermittent Fasting

In the prehistoric times, our hunter-gatherer ancestors had no option but to fast because they had food only when they achieved a good hunting session. On days when their hunt was unsuccessful, they would starve or simply eat what little berries or fruits they could gather. Unwittingly or otherwise, they reaped the benefits of fasting. They were muscular, sturdy and healthy and survived through some of the most difficult times in human history, battling wild animals, extreme climates, harsh living conditions etc.

The ancient civilizations including the Greeks, the Sumerians, the people of the Indus Valley Civilizations, the Egyptians, and others used fasting as a method of healing the body. Records that prove the use of 'starvation' to help in the recovery of a diseased or sick body and even as a preventive measure have been unearthed in many places. These ancient and wise civilizations were keenly aware of and employed the benefits of fasting and intermittent fasting to improve their health.

In many religions, fasting was used to reflect self-control and/or as a form of penitence. Let us look at some of the world religions and their deep connection to fasting:

Judaism – Yom Kippur or the Day of Atonement is the most popular day of fasting followed in Judaism. The Jews also fast on six other days each year including Tish B'Av, which is the day when their temples were destroyed.

Buddhism – Strict forms of fasting (that can potentially lead to starvation and death) are not part of Buddhism, which strongly advocates a 'middle path.' However, in most monasteries, monks eat only one meal a day (around noon time) as a way of staying healthy. Eating only one meal a day aids in meditation.

The average Buddhist fasts on certain days to understand the feeling of hunger, which helps in empathizing with people who don't have enough to eat. Fasting for Buddhism is done moderately in line with their core 'Middle Path' belief.

Christianity – Nearly all Christian sects fast during the 40-day Lent period that precedes Easter Sunday as a form of penitence and self-control. Christians follow various fasting methods including giving up meat, sacrificing certain luxuries, or one-meal-a-day fasting.

Hinduism – Fasting is a critical element of the Hindu religion. Some sects have practically one fasting day each week! There are fortnightly, monthly, and yearly fasting days too. Fasting in Hinduism is rooted in spirituality, health, and self-control and sacrifice.

Jainism – In the Jain religion, fasting is taken very seriously. In fact, even in modern times, many followers of the Jain religion have their last meal before 5 p.m. Additionally, there is a self-starvation ritual in Jainism referred to as 'Santhara' wherein the participant chooses voluntary death by starvation; perhaps, an extreme measure for the contemporary world. However, it reflects the seriousness with which fasting is treated in Jainism.

Islam – Fasting during the month of Ramadan is one of the 'Five Pillars' of the Islamic faith. Ramadan fasting calls for complete and absolute abstinence from food and drinks including water during daylight. You are allowed to eat only after sunset and before sunrise on all the days of the holy month.

Followers of Islam fast because they believe self-control and sacrifice get them closer to God. Moreover, Muslims believe that voluntary abstinence helps one understand and empathize with less fortunate people thereby increasing compassion and love for all mankind.

Interestingly, voluntary fasting was one of the most popular effective non-violent means employed by Mahatma Gandhi to fight for freedom from his country from the British. This great leader literally cajoled the British to leave India voluntary by using fasting methods multiple times to showcase his protest of their rule.

Understanding Breakfast, Lunch, and Dinner

During the ancient civilizations, breakfast was unheard of. The Greeks and Romans ate one meal around noontime not because there was a scarcity of food (these two civilizations thrived) but, because it was believed that eating one meal a day was good for health. Eating more than needed was not a sign of gluttony, thought the ancient wise men.

There is an interesting story to the famous 'bacon and eggs' breakfast that is a big hit in today's world. During the Middle Ages, on Monday and Tuesday preceding Ash Wednesday, people were compelled to exhaust the remains of meat and eggs as these items are not allowed to be consumed during Lent. As pork and bacon were the most commonly used meats in those days, the people then would cook them together which is believed to be the precursor of the modern-day bacon and eggs.

Around the 17th century, the aristocracy and the wealthy started consuming a morning meal, and called it breakfast for 'breaking the fast.' The fast here refers to not eating during the night because you were 'sleeping!' With the advent of the Industrial Revolution, there was an increasing number of workers working in factories putting in standard work hours from morning to night. These workers needed a substantial meal in the morning to sustain them throughout the day. Thus, breakfast began to be consumed by the common people.

John Harvey Kellogg created cornflakes in the beginning of the 20th century and revolutionized and popularized the concept of breakfast, and today, not necessarily for the correct reasons, most people believe that breakfast should never be missed. The explanation for this misplaced belief is explained in the later chapters of this book.

Now, coming to lunch, this meal seemed to always exist in human history though it was not called by the same name. People in nearly all civilizations had their primary meal of the day around noon. During the Industrial Revolution, factory workers toiled for over 6-8 hours at a stretch. The concept of 'luncheon' came into effect at this time, which gave these workers sustenance to carry on their strenuous labor for the rest of the day.

The evening/last meal of the day happened before sunset or before darkness set in. With the invention of artificial lighting, the inclusion of a substantial breakfast and lunch (which kept people not hungry enough for an early dinner), the evening meal got pushed to a later time than before and became the modern-day dinner.

By the end of the 18th century, people fit in three meals a day. This concept was more common in urban areas where factories flourished and working hours were structured and standardized. Therefore, before this period, 3-4 meals were unheard of, and yet people lived healthily. In fact, the concept of stress (which is closely related to food today) was almost absent until the beginning of the Industrial Revolution, which more or less standardized the concept of 'working hours' that stretched into long and laboriously monotonous ones.

Therefore, the intermittent fasting of today is not a new concept. It has been part of human history from ages ago, and we are only trying to give it a contemporary profile aligned with the lifestyle of today. Our ancestors just did the natural thing. We are trying to give a fanciful name, that's it.

Moreover, multiple scientific research studies only seem to reiterate the benefits that our ancestors already knew and took advantage of. The observations and biological inferences from these studies on intermittent fasting enhance our understanding of the way our body behaves for a positive impact; these benefits are not new, they were always there.

Read on, and find out more about how intermittent fasting works, and how you can leverage its multiple benefits including weight loss, improved physical fitness, improved levels of psychical and mental energy, increased resistance to illnesses, and more.

Chapter One: How Does Intermittent Fasting Work and What Are Its Benefits

Let's start understanding this intriguing subject by answer the most pertinent question, "What is intermittent fasting (IF)?"

As already explained in the introduction chapter, before the modern-day trend of having 3-4 meals a day started, our hunter-gatherer ancestors and the wise people of the ancient civilizations had only 1-2 meals. That is nothing but intermittent fasting. Switching between feasting and fasting is called intermittent fasting.

Intermittent fasting is not a diet. It is a pattern or method of eating. The most critical aspect of intermittent fasting is not on WHAT is eaten but WHEN it is eaten.

No major concern exists on micromanaging consumed nutrients as long as you are not overeating during your feeding period. Additionally, while processed and junk foods are to be avoided, all other nutrients including carbs, proteins, fats, etc. are not required to be measured and micromanaged to the last calorie which is what most crash diets expect you to do.

You choose the time of fasting and feasting based on your lifestyle and eating habits. The feasting time is the window in which you can eat your 1-2 meals, and the fasting time is the window when you fast. One of the simplest forms of intermittent fasting commonly used by beginners is to skip breakfast.

So, here's the scene: You have had your dinner at 8 p.m., and you skip breakfast the next day. Don't eat anything until your lunchtime, which is typically 12 noon. So, you have remained in the fasted state from 8 p.m. the previous night until 12 noon the next day which totals to 16 hours, and is known as the 16:8 type of intermittent fasting.

Similarly, there are other types of IF that you can choose from depending on your needs and lifestyle. The types of IF are discussed in Chapter Three.

How Does Intermittent Fasting Work?

Your body can exist only in two states namely fed and fasted states. In the fed state, the level of insulin in your blood rises. Insulin is a critical hormone that plays an important part in digestion. It is produced by the pancreas and is essential for the body to use glucose or sugar from consumed carbs for energy. Insulin is needed to balance the sugar level in your blood and to prevent hyperglycemia (a condition resulting from excessive sugar in the blood) and hypoglycemia (a condition resulting from dangerously low levels of sugar in the blood).

Nearly all the foods we consume except pure fat increase the level of insulin in your blood. Insulin is a nutrient sensor, and 'senses' the ingestion of carb- and protein-containing foods. Very few foods do not increase insulin production and release when they are consumed; pure fat is one such nutrient. On the other extreme, carbohydrates, and specifically processed carbs cause insulin to spike.

Now, your body needs a continuous supply for energy for its basic metabolism. Some of the critical metabolic activities, which require a constant supply of energy, include:

Pumping of blood by the heart

Detoxification functions of the liver and kidneys

The exhalation and inhalation functioning of the lungs

The functioning of the brain

Therefore, your body needs a supply of energy that is always available, no matter what. As we cannot keep eating all the time, the excess food we have consumed gets converted to energy and gets stored. In the fed state, the energy needed to carry out basic metabolism is taken from the ingested food. In the fasted state, this energy is taken from the stored food.

If you are going to supply your body with newly-ingested food at all times, it is never going to use the energy from the stored food, which is nothing but fat and glycogen stored in the liver (limited amount) and fat as adipose tissue all over the body (unlimited amount).

During intermittent fasting, the supply of energy from the ingested food gets exhausted, and the body is compelled to reach out and take the energy from the stored food, which primarily exists as fat in the body resulting in weight loss and multiple other benefits.

There is no one method of IF that suits everyone. The biggest advantage of using IF is that it is very flexible. You can choose the type that is most suitable for you. You can start with something as simple as fasting for 10-12 hours initially, and when your body gets adjusted to the new metabolism, then you can gradually increase the intensity by increasing the duration of the fasting window.

Understanding Human Metabolism

We need to understand human metabolism in a little more detail to know how IF benefits us immensely. Nearly all our foods are a combination of three macronutrients namely carbohydrates, proteins, and fats.

The foods we eat have these macronutrients in varying compositions. While some foods such as rice, pasta, bread, potato, and others have a higher percentage of carbs, some other foods such as legumes, lean meats, etc. have a higher amount of proteins, and some others such as red meats, oils, etc. have high amounts of fats.

The process of metabolism begins when we start consuming food. It starts with the breakdown of macronutrients into its component parts, and continues until the energy released is either used up or stored in the body. Carbohydrates get converted to glucose or simple sugar. Proteins are broken down into amino acids. Fats become fatty acids and glycerol. These components are further converted into energy for immediate needs, and the excess amounts are stored as energy reserves in various parts of the body. Here is a short summary of what happens to each component parts of each of the macronutrients during metabolism:

Glucose – After a meal, the blood glucose level quickly rises resulting in the production of insulin. Insulin transfers the glucose from the blood to the cells, tissues, and muscles of your body where it is used for energy. The glucose that is not immediately required gets converted into glycogen and is in your muscles and liver. However, the amount of glycogen that can be stored in these two places is limited, and, therefore, any glucose in excess of this amount gets converted to fat and is stored as adipose tissues all over your body. Typically, glucose is the primary source of fuel for your body.

Amino acids – Amino acids are the end-products of protein metabolism. They are needed for repair and maintenance of cells and tissues. Amino acids are also necessary for the synthesis of new cells. The normal adult body needs very few amino acids for repair and maintenance. Therefore, the excess is converted into glucose by the liver which again goes through the process of getting stored as glycogen in the liver and muscle, and when the glycogen accumulation level is breached, it gets converted into fat and is stored as adipose tissue all over the body.

Fatty acids – It is highly unlikely that fatty acids from fats will be needed for immediate use as most of the energy needed for basic metabolism is obtained from the glucose of the supplied food (especially during fed state). Some amount of fatty acids along with amino acids are used for repair and maintenance. Therefore, the fatty acids get converted to fats and stored in adipose tissue as stored energy for use when energy from the fed state is exhausted completely.

For several hours after eating, your body is busy converting all the excess food you have eaten into stored energy for later use. This is the fed state. When the storage process is completed, then your body gets into the fasted state, and at the beginning of this state, your fuel stores do not get any added fuel. Instead, fuel from this stored energy is used up by the body.

The longer you put your body in the fasted state, the more fuel from the stored energy is used up releasing the fat loss.

A Scientific Explanation of Intermittent Fasting

The body's energy sources come in the form of glucose and fats. Glucose is easier to burn than fat and, therefore, in a fed state (when there is a continuous supply of glucose from the consumed food), the body chooses to burn sugars for its energy needs instead of fat. Fats along with excess amino acids and glucose get stored as adipose or fat tissues for use in the absence of glucose.

Primarily, intermittent fasting drives your body to access the energy needed for its requirements from stored fat because you have deliberately cut off the supply of food that would otherwise have come from the 3-4 meals consumed each day. Stored fat is nothing but fuel energy that can be used by the body when its default 'preferred' form of fuel (typically glucose or sugar) is not available.

Again, excess energy from consumed food is stored in two ways in the body. First, excess glucose gets converted to glycogen and is kept in the liver and muscles. These places have limited amounts of storage space, like your refrigerator. Storing and accessible energy in this 'refrigerator' is easy.

But, because of the limited space, the body cannot store much here. Therefore, any additional energy in the form of glucose or amino acids or fatty acids get converted into fats and stored in adipose tissues all over the body. The body is similar to a large-sized industrial-grade freezer, which can store humongous amounts of food energy. Storing this kind of food energy is difficult, and accessing it is even more difficult.

So, to summarize, stored energy in your body is available in two forms; the easily accessible but limited amount of glycogen in the liver and muscles, and the not-so-easily accessible but an unlimited supply of fat in the adipose tissues.

During the fasting state, the blood-insulin levels fall triggering the body to reach out for stored energy for its fuel needs because there is no energy supply from consumed food. So, the body will first reach out for glycogen from the liver and muscles. On sustained fasting, this limited supply of glycogen will also be exhausted, and that is when the body reaches out to stored fat for its energy supply.

It takes at least 12 hours of being in the fasting state for the body to use a significant amount of fat for its energy needs. The longer you extend the fasting window, the more energy is used up by the body from the stored fat cells. Exercising and remaining physically active during the fasting state helps to increase the rate of fat burn.

Some people are more prone to get into the fat-burning mode faster and more effectively than others. This biological tendency is referred to as 'metabolic flexibility.' The good thing about 'metabolic flexibility' is that it works like a muscle; the more you work at it, the more flexible and stronger it will become. Therefore, after a few weeks of practicing intermittent fasting, your body's metabolic flexibility will increase, and you will be able to burn fat faster and more effectively than before.

In the fasting state, the body uses a combination of the following forms of fuel for all its energy purposes:

Fatty acids that are released from adipose tissues or body fat

Ketones from the fatty acids produced by the liver

Glucose from glycogen

So, why does the body need this combination of fuel sources? Because different physiological and biological functions performed by different organs and tissues need different kinds of fuels for optimal functioning. Here are a few examples:

Muscles can use energy from fatty acids or glucose obtained from their stored glycogen to work efficiently.

The heart works efficiently with energy from fatty acids.

Nerves and the brain typically need glucose energy for optimal functioning; they can also work well with ketones.

RBCs or red blood cells can work only with energy from glucose.

Even in the fasting state, your body's excellent energy mechanism can maintain sufficient levels of blood-glucose for RBCs to perform at their peak levels. The brain can extract glucose from glycogen through glycogenolysis, and the liver can synthesize new glucose molecules by breaking down stored fats and amino acids.

Difference between Intermittent Fasting and Starvation

One of the most significant misconceptions about intermittent fasting is that it is likened to starvation. Even those who are keenly interested in giving it a try are worried that they will get into starvation mode in which muscle gets converted into energy resulting in muscle loss. Here are some myth-busting points that will help you understand the difference better:

Myth #1 – Why does our store the excess food as fat? – So as to use this stored energy during times of food shortage. Let us use the example of our hunter-gatherer ancestors again. During summers, they got a lot of food, ate well, and become healthier. Going out to hunt during winters was foolhardy, and so our wise ancestors stayed indoors with little or no access to food resulting in voluntary fasting.

How did they survive these winters then? Their bodies used up the stored fats for energy needs. If during fasting, muscles were used instead of fat, our ancestors would have had round tummies and thin hands and legs, right? This was not the case. Moreover, why would our body store fat for future use, and use up muscle when the time comes? This argument is quite contrary to the way nature works. Therefore, muscles do not waste away during fasting.

When all the fat has been used up by the body, and even then there was no food, it would reach out into muscles for its energy needs, but not until then.

Myth #2 – Muscles are the first energy reserves that our body uses in the absence of food – To understand this, we need to understand why our body builds muscles. Muscles are built and maintained for strength. Let us go back to our ancestors. If muscles instead of fat were broken down for regular energy needs, then our ancestors would not have had the strength to survive the winter, and come out at the other end, ready for a new kill so that their families could get food.

Using up muscles weakens the body, which is against the natural survival instinct of all living beings.

So, let us end this argument with the following basic difference between starvation and fasting:

Fasting is the voluntary abstinence of foods during which our body uses stored fat for its energy needs. There is no lack of essential nutrients to do normal work.

Starvation, on the other hand, is a state when essential nutrients needed to support life.

Benefits of Intermittent Fasting

Now, that you know how naturally intermittent fasting works, let us look at some of its benefits.

Weight Loss

Although Chapter Five talks about weight loss in a bit more detail, as this is one of the biggest benefits of IF, it would be unfair not to mention it (at least briefly) in this section. Fasting ensures your source of glucose is completely drained out so that your body switches into fat-burning mode resulting in effective weight loss. Moreover, studies proved that an occasional brief break from intermittent fasting does not really impact your progress negatively.

The best part of weight loss from intermittent fasting is that your belly fat is reduced considerably. When your body burns fat, it reaches out to all parts for stored fat including the adamant belly fat. Thus, if you sustain your efforts at intermittent fasting, your belly fat will also dissolve.

Reduces Insulin Resistance

One of the most common diseases of modern times is Type 2 diabetes, which is characterized by increased insulin resistance. Therefore, any therapy that reduces the level of insulin in the blood can help in controlling type 2 diabetes. Intermittent fasting is known to impact insulin resistance positively thereby reducing the risk of Type 2 diabetes. Some studies revealed that men were more likely to be benefited than women.

Reduces Inflammation and Oxidative Stress

Oxidative stress is characterized by the presence of harmful free radicals that are unstable and can react with and damage other critical molecules in the body such as proteins and DNA. Based on various scientific studies, experts opine that intermittent fasting improves the body's resistance to oxidative stress, which, in turn, reduces the risk of multiple diseases and illnesses caused by oxidative stress.

Additionally, intermittent fasting is also known the increase the body's capability to fight against inflammation, a huge risk factor for many common disorders. Reduced oxidative stress and the decrease of chronic inflammation from intermittent fasting can also improve the texture of your skin as damaging free radicals become less than before. This also helps to clear acne and pimples from your face.

Improves Brain Functioning

Advancing age restricts blood flow to the brain resulting in the shrinkage of neurons and reduction in brain volume. IF stems the process of aging, and keeps you mentally alert and sharp. Here are some ways that IF boosts your brain functioning:

Promotes autophagy and prevents degeneration of neurons – Intermittent fasting promotes autophagy in the brain. Autophagy is the body's natural process to clean out damaged cells and replace them with newly generated cells. IF promotes autophagy specifically in the neurons of the brain thereby facilitating improved defense against brain-related disorders. IF protects neurons from degeneration and death. IF is known to help guard neurons found in the brain from neuronal death or excitotoxic stress.

Lowers risk of multiple diseases – IF promotes brain health and thereby reduces the risk of brain-related disorders such as Parkinson's and Alzheimer's. Moreover, intermittent fasting helps in weight reduction and therefore facilitates reduced obesity, and helps in fighting against diabetes; both these conditions increase the risk of Alzheimer's.

Reduces depression – Multiple studies have revealed that when people suffering from depression resorted to intermittent fasting, there was a marked improvement in their moods, calmness and mental alertness.

Boosts memory – Studies have proven that IF helps to boost learning and memory, which, in turn, helps, protect the brain against severe neurodegenerative diseases.

Improves Heart Health

Intermittent fasting has shown to improve heart health by positively impacting and regulating multiple risk factors associated with heart disease including LDL and total cholesterol, blood pressure, inflammatory markers, blood triglycerides, and, of course, blood sugar levels.

Promotes Longevity

In addition to reducing insulin resistance, lowering cholesterol levels, and improving brain functioning (all of which contribute to improving longevity), intermittent fasting also reduces the risk of the following deadly diseases and risk factors resulting in improved longevity:

Slows down cancer growth – Multiple studies have revealed that when intermittent fasting is done in combination with chemotherapy, then the progression of skin cancer and breast cancer can be slowed down. This happens because IF is believed to enhance lymphocytes that attack and kill cancer cells.

Slows down the aging process – By reducing oxidative stress and inflammation, intermittent fasting is known to slow down the aging process thereby enhancing longevity. Intermittent fasting is known to manipulate the cellular power generators or the mitochondrial network. These mitochondria were observed to be fused together in study participants who were doing intermittent fasting. Fusing together helped increase the power of the mitochondrial network resulting in their improved productivity and efficiency. This meant that cells got increased energy and became vibrant which, in turn, resulting in improved health and slowing down of the aging process.

Improves Energy and Productivity

Overeating and eating excessive refined foods make us tired and weak. Ask yourself how you feel after a heavy meal. Sleepy, tired, and completely unenergetic, right? That is what overconsumption of food does to your body. Fasting, on the other hand, keeps your mind alert and sharp and improves your powers of focus and concentration.

What happens during fasting is this. The digestive system does not need any energy as there is no food for it to work on. Therefore, this energy is 'freed up' and is used for other productive work by your body including improving brain function, repair and maintenance of cells and tissues, etc.

Improved brain function translates into enhanced cognitive powers thereby rendering you more alert and capable of greater mental accuracy. Fasting also makes you feel lighter and more energetic because, during fasting, your body gets its energy from fat and not glucose. One gram of fat releases 9 calories as against 4 calories from one gram of glucose. Therefore, your energy levels go up with intermittent fasting.

Additionally, intermittent fasting increases the production and release of growth hormone. This hormone is vital for the preservation of muscle mass and bone density. It also helps in promoting fat metabolism and is also needed for cell growth and repair. Growth hormone production reduces with advancing age. Intermittent fasting is believed to be one of the most effective ways to triggering the production of this critical hormone.

Improved Taste Sensitivity

Eating salty, sugary, and processed foods desensitize our taste buds to the subtle flavors of natural, wholesome foods. Our taste buds are used to excessive flavors and lose the ability to identify natural flavors. After a couple of fasting periods, your taste buds functions are reset to their natural levels, and you will be able to appreciate and savor earthy, wholesome, and subtle flavors. In fact, after some weeks into intermittent fasting, you could find yourself becoming allergic to overpowering flavors like those found in junk and processed foods.

Simplifies Your Life

And finally, intermittent fasting simplifies your life because you don't need to worry about your meals as often as before. You just have to plan for 2 slightly large meals, and one little snack. In fact, after you have gained experience with IF, and extend your fasting window even more than before, you will notice you have a lot of time in your hands as meal-planning, spending time eating your meals, and other food and cooking related activities reduce time considerably. Your life becomes simple, easy, and free, leaving you more time and energy to do the things you love.

Improved Willpower and Self-Confidence

Intermittent fasting calls for strong willpower to battle against ever-assailing food temptations that surround you. Moreover, you need strong willpower to fight against hunger pangs, cravings and other psychological temptations as well. With each battle, the strength of your willpower improves, and you find it increasingly easy to resist temptations of all kinds and be disciplined to your IF cause.

When you notice the tangible results of this increased willpower in the form of compliments from friends and family on your weight loss, on the improvement of your skin texture, increased energy, etc. your level of self-confidence also goes up. You enjoy the victory of surmounting multiple challenges that you encounter to achieve your goal successfully. This self-confidence spreads to other personal and professional aspects of your life too.

Chapter Two: Some Myths Busted and Who Should Avoid Intermittent Fasting

There are multiple misconceived and unsubstantiated myths floating around regarding intermittent fasting. Before we go further, it makes sense to bust some of these myths, and also let you know some contraindications and precautions that need to be taken for certain individuals. So, let's go bust some myths:

Myth #1 – Breakfast Is the Most Important and Un-missable Meal of the Day

Most of us have been brainwashed into believing that breakfast is the most important meal of the day and that without it, you are going to feel fatigued resulting in unproductivity, inefficiency, and also, bingeing during lunch time. This advice is quite misplaced.

When you wake up in the morning, your body has just about reached the fasted state (after nearly 10-12 hours after the last meal). Insulin and glucose levels are low, and your body has begun to reach out to stored fat for its energy needs. Now, when you eat breakfast, your fat-burning comes to an immediate halt, which is counterproductive to weight loss, and multiple other benefits of IF. Instead, if you simply skipped your morning breakfast, then your body will go into an intense fat-burning state.

Eating a high-carb breakfast is the worst scenario because both insulin and glucose levels will spike, and your body will get out of the fasted state almost immediately. Not only does eating breakfast spike insulin and glucose levels, and shut off the fat-burning process but also a lot more needless calories get accumulated as fat again. Additionally, later on during the morning, you will see huge drops in glucose levels, which is the perfect trigger for hunger resulting in increased cravings.

As your body gets into the fat-burning mode faster and more effectively than before, you will notice that you hardly get hungry in the mornings. You also don't feel any kind of excessive cravings before your lunchtime, and yet you will have adequate energy to perform all your activities efficiently and productively. Our ancestors, wittingly or unwittingly, followed this exact lifestyle. They went out early in the morning (on an empty stomach) to hunt for food and gather wild berries, and came back home in the late afternoon or early evening to eat one big satiating meal of the day!

So, the idea that skipping breakfast is bad for health is a myth because the biological processes confirm quite the opposite. In fact, multiple research studies have revealed results that counter earlier observations that eating breakfast is good for obesity reduction. Therefore, as a beginner in intermittent fasting, skipping breakfast is one of the easiest and most effective ways to begin your IF journey as a large portion of the fasting window is covered during your sleep time.

Myth #2 - Intermittent Fasting Results in Low Blood-Sugar of Hypoglycemia

Multiple studies have proven that normal individuals who are not suffering from any ailments and who are not taking medication for diabetes can fast for long periods of time without any negative impact on blood-sugar levels. In fact, in nearly all non-diabetics, it is seen that hypoglycemia sets in when excessive carbs are consumed. Here is what happens when high-carb foods are consumed frequently:

Blood-glucose spikes

Blood-insulin spikes

Blood-glucose drops significantly (hypoglycemia sets in) after some time while insulin remains at more or less the same level

Cravings set in driving you to eat more

Diabetics on medication will have to necessarily check with their physicians before starting off intermittent fasting.

Myth #3 - Intermittent Fasting Slows Down Metabolism

This is also a complete myth. Multiple studies have shown that there is no effect on metabolism even when fasting is carried out for 72 hours. On the contrary, fasting could marginally increase metabolism driven by the increased release of catecholamines such as adrenaline or epinephrine, dopamine, and norepinephrine.

Further, fasting activates the sympathetic nervous system that is known for fight/flight response; another key element to increase metabolism. And this makes a lot of sense because our hunter-gatherer ancestors needed the fight-flight response to work at its peak when they hunted, and the 'rest and digest' (driven by the parasympathetic nerves) mode activated at night.

Therefore, IF slowing down metabolism is wrong.

Myth #4 - Intermittent Fasting Leads to Muscle Loss

Another common misconception about intermittent fasting is that people think they will lose muscle when they fast. However, nothing is further from the truth because the growth hormone level is significantly increased during fasted states. Studies have shown that growth hormone rises nearly 2000% after 24 hours of fasting.

So, why is growth hormone significant for muscle? Because it is anabolic, which means it, builds muscles. Bodybuilders combine growth hormone with testosterone in their health drinks to result in the dual advantage of building muscle and losing fat. The level of growth hormone increases during fast to facilitate muscle preservation.

It is for this reason that our hunter-gatherer ancestors (who were driven to fasting because of a shortage of food) became stronger with each generation. If fasting made you weaker, human beings would not have survived and thrived for so many millennia.

Not only is muscle preserved during fasting but if combined with strength training, muscles can even grow. Also, during fasting, our alertness levels are very high driven by the release of epinephrine and norepinephrine.

Myth #5 – Eating Small Meals Frequently Is Healthy Whereas Eating Fewer Large-Sized Meals Is Not

Eating frequent small meals is believed to keep the metabolism going, and keeping your body is a fasting or starvation mode reduces metabolism. This is a complete myth. Fat burning is what increasing metabolism, and to burn fat, you must remain in the fasted state for a long time.

The more frequently you feed your body, the less time it will remain in a fasted state. In fact, if your meals are very frequent, no matter who small your meals are, your body will always have access to glucose for its energy, and will never reach out to its stored fat for its energy needs.

The more frequent your meals, the less efficient your body will be when it comes to burning fat. The longer the duration of fasting state, the more efficient your body becomes in burning fat. Additionally, we have been told that proteins need to be supplied to the body through frequent meals. This idea has no scientific basis. Yes, an adequate amount of proteins is needed for healthy muscles. However, there is no requirement for frequent supply of this nutrient.

Who can benefit from intermittent fasting? Nearly anyone and everyone can benefit from the intermittent fasting. Here is a short summary of the benefits of IF discussed in Chapter One, and a few more:

Promotes fat and weight loss

Enhances insulin sensitivity

Improves metabolism

Promotes longevity

Improves brain functioning

Reduces risks of neurodegenerative diseases

Increased resistance to hunger pangs

Improves your ability to appreciate wholesome foods

Improves eating patterns

Rests the digestive system

If you want to leverage the above benefits and more, you can start intermittent fasting by choosing the method that is most suitable for you. However, there are a few contraindications and precautions for certain individuals. In fact, for certain people, IF is strictly forbidden. Here are a few examples of people who should avoid intermittent fasting unless prescribed by a qualified physician.

Who Should Not Try Intermittent Fasting?

Pregnant women and lactating mothers; they need extra energy and, therefore, experimenting with intermittent fasting at this time is prohibited for health reasons.

People with a history of eating disorders; for such people, it is important to set their eating patterns in order first, and then jump into intermittent fasting.

People suffering from chronic stress; in the initial days of intermittent fasting, there could be some amount of stress considering the change in lifestyle that you are adopting. Therefore, people with chronic stress issues could end up complicating their problems even further and should avoid IF.

People with insomnia issues. Insomnia also creates a lot of stress, and IF should be avoided for the same reasons as for people with chronic stress.

Other than the above set of people, typically, intermittent fasting can be tried by everyone else. However, it is always a good thing to speak to a qualified physician, and take his or her opinion to ensure you are doing the right thing for you.

Chapter Three: Methods of Intermittent Fasting

As you know by now that intermittent fasting involves abstaining from eating for predetermined periods of time alternated with periods of eating. The duration when you don't eat is called the fasting window, and the duration when you eat is called the eating window.

One of the biggest advantages of intermittent fasting is that there are multiple variations available, and you can choose what suits you the best. So, let us look at some of the methods of intermittent fasting along with critical research observations for each of them.

Intermittent Fasting #1: Random Meal Skipping

This method is great for beginners where you simply choose to randomly skip meals depending on the intensity of your hunger or time restraints or any other reason. Again, it is important not to overeat at the next meal.

This method is likely to be successful for people who monitor their hunger pangs and respond appropriately to them. Such people eat when they are hungry, and skip meals when they are not hungry. For some people, this appears to be a more natural method of intermittent fasting than the others. There is no formal pattern to be followed.

Intermittent Fasting #2: 12:12 Method - 12-Hour Fasting Window and 12-Hour Eating Window

This is, perhaps, the simplest and easiest method for beginners to take their first step into the world of intermittent fasting. In this method, you can choose two fixed 12-hour periods for eating and fasting. Some research studies have observed that the body begins to burn fat after fasting for 10-16 hours.

Therefore, fasting for 12 hours can potentially give the body a 2-hour window for fat-burning. Some studies have proven the efficacy of this intermittent fasting method in weight loss. The reason why this method is great for beginners is that the fasting duration is relatively small (only 12 hours) out of which about 6-8 hours coincide with your sleeping time; if the fasting duration is chosen sensibly. In this method, the beginner can eat the same amount of calories as before.

For example, you can choose the fasting window to be between 8 p.m. and 8 a.m. So, ensure you finish your dinner before 8 in the evening, and have your breakfast after 8 the next morning. The other meals of the day can remain the same for you.

For many beginners, this would be a perfect way to start because prior to this, the fasting window would ideally have been between 8 and 10 hours. For example, typically, most of us (who are not into IF) have our dinner at around 10 p.m., and the next meal would be breakfast at around 8 a.m. leaving a fasting window of 10 hours. With the 12-hour IF method, you would only need to extend the fasting time by 2 hours which is not very difficult to do.

Once your body and mind get used to the concept of fasting, then you can extend the fasting window to the next method, which is 16:8 method.

Pros – It is very easy to follow this method as you only need to extend your fasting period by a couple of hours.

Cons – The beneficial effects of IF may not show through this method because fat-burning is restricted to only 2 hours.

Intermittent Fasting #3: 16:8 Method – 16-Hour Fasting Window and 8-Hour Eating Window

This method is called the Leangains Method where you fast for 16 hours (for men) and 14 hours (for women) at a stretch and eat in the remaining 8-10-hour window. You can move into this method after you have tried the 12:12 option and found that either it did not work for you or it worked for some time, and now you have plateaued.

Typically in this method, you should finish your dinner before 8 p.m., skip breakfast the next morning, and eat your lunch, which will be the first meal of the day.

Multiple studies conducted on mice using this method revealed great results in the fight against obesity, and protection against liver disease, diabetes and inflammation.

Skipping breakfast is not bad for your health. The myth surrounding breakfast was broken down in Chapter Two. Here are some more great reasons why missing breakfast is actually a good thing:

Skipping breakfast does not affect your metabolism negatively – Studies have shown that missing out on breakfast does not slow down your metabolism. Metabolism is driven by physical activity, the base metabolic rate, and the energy used to digest food. Metabolism is a continuous process that takes place 24/7 and does not depend on any meal. Therefore, if you are eating breakfast in the morning only on the assumption that otherwise, your metabolism will suffer, you can stop right now.

Eating breakfast does not aid weight loss – In multiple studies, it was observed that weight loss was affected by eating breakfast. The people who ate breakfast lost weight to the same extent as people who skipped breakfast with other factors remaining common.

Your brain continues to work efficiently even if there is no food in your stomach – It is a common misconception that not having food in the stomach reduces the efficiency of the brain. Our brain is too sophisticated an organ to depend on food in the stomach for its functioning. There are multiple other energy sources it draws its needed calories from for its efficient functioning. Therefore, there is no need to fill up your empty stomach with breakfast as soon as you wake up.

Skipping breakfast is not essential for the 16:8 method. You can choose to eat your dinner or your last meal of the day at 4 p.m., which will also give you the same, 16:8 fasting and feasting windows. Sugarless coffee, tea, and other calorie-free drinks are fine in the fasting window. A bit of milk in your coffee and tea is fine too. This method is easily adaptable into any kind of lifestyle. The trick is to keep the feeding window consistent to prevent hormones from being unbalanced.

Pros – It is easy to maintain this method because you can eat whenever you want during the 8-hour feeding window. Most people prefer breaking their nutritional requirements into three different meals in the 8-hour window.

Cons – You can eat whenever you want during the 8-hour eating window. However, there are some fairly strict guidelines as to what you can and what you cannot eat for this method, especially if you are working out. Moreover, if you eat three meals in 8 hours, then it is quite likely to consume more calories than needed; a situation, which is counterproductive to weight loss. It requires you to maintain a strict eye over what you eat in this method.

Intermittent Fasting #4: 5:2 Method – Fast for Two Days, and Eat Normally for 5 Days of the Week

The 5:2 intermittent fasting method also called the Fast Diet works like this:

Men eat 600 calories, and women consume 500 calories on 2 days of the week

Eat normally on 5 days of the week

The reduced calorie intake on the two days can potentially result in a lot of fat loss. However, it is imperative that you don't binge-eat on the normal-feeding days. There should be at least a one-day gap between the two fasting days. Here is an example:

Reduced calorie intake on Mondays and Thursdays

Normal calorie intake on the other days

You can choose any two days of your convenience. You only have to remember to keep a gap of one day between the two days when calorie-restriction is enforced. Also, it is important that normal eating days does not mean you can eat anything and everything you want. You must eat as if you didn't fast at all.

Moreover, the choice of foods for IF, although not restricted excessively unlike other diets, play an important part for success. Chapter Six discusses the foods that should be avoided and to be included in IF.

Some studies focused on the 5:2 method showed that it was possible to control obesity to the same extent in this way as by restricting calorie intake continuously.

Pros – You will have to restrict food intake only on two days and this can be easier to maintain than having to fast continuously on all days even if it is only for 16 hours.

Cons – Some people could find it difficult to work normally with only 500-600 calorie intake.

Intermittent Fasting #5: The Eat-Stop-Eat Method – Fasting for 24 Hours Once or Twice Every Week

This method calls for complete fasting for 24 hours at a stretch to be done once or twice a week. People fast from dinner to dinner or breakfast to breakfast or lunch to lunch giving their digestive systems a break for 24 hours. You can choose the 24-hour slot as per your needs and comfort levels. During the 24 hours, you cannot consume any foods though liquids in the form of sugar-free tea, coffee, water, and other calorie-free beverages are allowed.

On the non-fasting days, you can eat normally remembering to consume food as if you did not fast. Binge-eating after the day of a fast defeats the very purpose of fasting. So, you reduce the total calorie intake for the week while having the freedom to consume what you normally like.

Pros – Yes, for some of us, 24 hours might seem like a long period to stay without food. However, you don't have to start with 24 hours. Begin the fasting day with the intention of staying off food for 24 hours. Try and fast for as long as you feel comfortable in the initial stages. Increase the duration of your fasting period gradually over time until you reach the maximum 24 hours. Therefore, the biggest advantage of this method lies in its flexibility. Start slow and increase in small bouts.

Another great thing about the Fast Diet is that there are really no 'forbidden foods.' You can eat what you love to eat providing you don't make up for the fasting day calorie loss.

Cons – In the initial days, fasting for 24 hours could be a stretch for some people. They usually cite reasons like fatigues, headaches, crankiness, irritation, etc., and typically give up without much resistance. Initial periods of uneasiness are expected when you start your intermittent fasting journey. However, these discomforts are temporary in nature and disappear once your body gets accustomed to the new eating pattern.

Additionally, the long fasting period also enhances people's temptations to binge-eat after its completion. A lot of self-control is needed to eat only the normal amount of food after fasting for 24 hours, which could be a huge challenge for many.

Intermittent Fasting #6: The 18:6 Method – Fasting for 18 Hours and Feeding for 6 Hours

Once you are comfortable with the 16:8 method, you can slowly increase your fasting period to 18 hours. This is typically the best form of intermittent fasting to achieve for beginners. The fat burning state exists for about 6-8 hours resulting in optimum lipolysis efficiency.

Like the 16:8 method, this type also calls for skipping breakfast, a light lunch at around noon, a little snack at 3 p.m., and dinner (the last meal of the day at 6 in the evening) which will leave you a fasting period of 18 hours until the next day's lunch. A major difference between the 16:8 and 18:6 methods is an early dinner, typically not later than 6 p.m. Move to this method from the 16:8 method if you have plateaued there, and you are bound to see some great benefits.

Pros and Cons for the 18:6 method are the same as the 16:8 method except that it might be a struggle (at least initially) to fast for 18 hours a stretch. But, once your body gets used to it, you can keep this pattern of eating for the rest of your life to achieve weight loss and leverage the other IF benefits optimally.

Intermittent Fasting #7 – The Warrior Diet – Fasting for 20 Hours and Feeding for 4 Hours

This is perfect for you once you have perfected the art of intermittent fasting, and your body and mind are ready to take on the extreme challenge. The Warrior Diet calls for a fasting period of 20 hours and a feeding window of 4 hours with a large meal at night. This method also requires you to watch what you eat and when you eat. The concept behind the Warrior Diet is that the human species consists of nocturnal eaters or those whose bodies are naturally programmed to eat one large meal at night. This method, therefore, is designed to align with our body's circadian rhythm.

The fasting window in this method actually translates to eating very little and can include small servings of raw vegetables, fruit, fresh fruit juices, and pure protein foods. All these foods are known to optimize the working of the sympathetic nervous system (responsible for the fight/flight mode), which, in turn, increases our sharpness and alertness, promotes burning of fat, and boosts energy requirements during the day.

The 4-hour eating window closer to dinnertime is designed to activate the parasympathetic nervous system (responsible for rest and relaxation) promoting calmness, efficient digestion and nutrient absorption, and relaxation while allowing the body to use the nutrients for repair, growth and maintenance of cells and tissues.

Eating during the 4-hour feeding window also has a method to be followed. You have to start with vegetables followed by proteins, and then fat. After finishing all these nutrient groups if you are still hungry, then you can add on some amount of carbs.

Pros – One of the most significant pros of the Warrior Diet is that it allows for small snacking (of course, restricted to raw fruit and veggies) thereby making it easier to go through the 20-hour fasting period. There is undoubtedly increased energy levels and a significant amount of fat burning that takes place in your body when you follow this method of intermittent fasting.

Cons – Although small snacks in the form of raw fruit and vegetables and fresh fruit juices are allowed, it can be quite challenging for many people to stay away from conventional food for such a long duration of time. That's why it's called a Warrior Diet; it's only doable by warriors of the intermittent fasting world. Yet, if you do manage to achieve this status, then this method is one of the most effective methods of fat loss and muscle building.

Intermittent Fasting #8 – Alternate Day Fasting

So, you fast one day and eat normally on the next day. Alternate eating and fasting days. This method of intermittent fasting has two variations. In one, people do not eat any solid food on the fasting day and eat as much as they want on the feeding day. In the second variation, people choose to restrict their calorie intake to 500 (for women) and 600 (for men) on the fasting days and eat normally on the feeding days.

Studies have shown that this method of IF is very effective for weight loss and improved heart health. This is quite an extreme form of fasting and may not be suitable for beginners and people with certain medical conditions. Yet, if weight loss is your goal, then this is the most efficient form to follow.

This method is ideal to try out carb cycling for effective carb management. What is carb cycling? It is a relatively new but effective dietary approach where you intentionally vary your carbohydrate intake so that some days are low-carb days and some are high-carb days.

In our efforts to reduce carbohydrate intake, many of us lose out on the multiple benefits of this important macronutrient. Excessive restriction of carbs can lead to reduced metabolism and hormonal imbalance. This is especially crucial for women for whom hormonal imbalances can result in weight loss plateauing. During such times, and to ensure you get a healthy dose of carbs into your system, carb cycling can be used.

In this method, for example, you can have one feeding day as a high-carb day, and the next feeding day as a low-carb day. Please note that carb cycling can also be done on a daily basis. For example, in the 16:8 method, you can choose one high-carb meal while the remaining one or two are low-carb meals. Carb cycling can also weekly or monthly too.

The benefit of carb cycling is that you allow your body to get sufficient supply of this important nutrient, and yet manage to keep carb consumption in check.

Pros – As already mentioned, it is most suited for you if weight loss is your main goal. If you can cut down weekly calorie intake by 20-35%, then you can potentially lose up to 2.5 pounds each week!

Cons – It is an extreme form of IF not because it is not easy to fast on fasting day but because it is quite easy to binge-eat on normal days repeatedly resulting in weight gain instead of weight loss. It is a tricky form to follow. The best ways to ensure you don't binge-eat on normal days is to have meals planned ahead so that you know what you will eat, and stick to that more strictly than if you didn't have a meal plan in place.

Choose your style of intermittent fasting, and most importantly, remember to take it gradually.

Some Self-Assessment Questions Before You Plunge In?

Q1. Do you get irritable and angry when you are hungry?

If the answer to the above question is a yes, then maybe, intermittent fasting is not really for you. If you are irritable when you are hungry, then IF might be a bad idea not just for you but for those around you as well. You might want to start really slowly by skipping random meals (especially when you are not hungry), and when you have learned to manage your hunger pangs better, then you can move on to the more difficult methods. If you realize you cannot manage your hunger-triggered anger, then it is best to avoid IF.

Q2. Do you use cheat meals to stay on course?

If the answer to this is a yes, then intermittent fasting will work really well for you. For example, if an ice-cream treat on the normal eating day is sufficient to prevent you from eating on the fasting day of the alternate day method, and IF is your cup of tea. Because IF is nothing but cutting down calories on certain days and eating your normal foods on other days. Yet, it makes sense to remind you that feeding days cannot be 'binge-eating' days, especially on unhealthy and processed foods. Then, you are bound to put on weight instead of losing weight!

Q3. Have you checked with your doctor?

While intermittent fasting is relatively safe because it is the most natural thing to do (after all, we are fasting when we sleep every night), sudden long periods of fasting can send your physiological system into a shock, especially if you have an underlying medical condition. Therefore, it is wise to speak to your physician or at least let him know about your plan before you get in. Please reread Chapter Two to know who should avoid IF.

Q4. Do you have an eating disorder?

Intermittent fasting helps you become more appreciative of wholesome foods as fasting periods will allow you saturated (with excessive flavors of processed foods) taste buds to regain some of their lost ability to discern and enjoy subtle flavors. Therefore, it is easy to plan and consume healthy balanced meals between fasting periods for optimum benefit. However, if you have an eating disorder already in place, then intermittent fasting could exacerbate your problems. It is best to avoid it.

Reread the different methods of intermittent fasting, the pros and cons and ask yourself some basic questions, ensure you do not belong to the set of people for whom IF is not recommended, and then take the plunge, and enjoy the benefits of intermittent fasting.

Chapter Four: Tips to Start off, what to Expect in the Initial Days and How to Manage Them

Tips Before You Start Off

Before you start off on your intermittent journey, ready your body and mind with the following tips:

Build your knowledge levels – Remember you will not die if you fast for a few hours. No one can die considering that the human body will is filled with reserve energy to help us survive for up to 30 days even if we did not consume even an ounce of food. Arm yourself with all the required information as to what will happen in your body, how the body will react and behave in the absence of food consumption, and other relevant information.

Read up books like this one, a lot of articles that answer any specific query you may have, and ask people who have used this form of diet and found success. Gather as much information as you can about intermittent fasting. Knowledge is power and armed with this power, you will not feel fear or any kind of burden when you undergo certain expected discomforts at the beginning of your IF journey.

If you start with a closed mind or an antagonistic feeling towards IF, your body and mind are going to resist all your efforts, and it will end in failure.

Feast before your fasting period – Suppose you have chosen to use the 16:8 fasting method and your last meal of the day is going to be at 8 p.m. after which you will be on a 16-hour fasting period. Ensure you have a nutritious and satiating meal at 8 p.m. In fact, eat enough for that 'I'm not going to ever eat a meal again,' feeling to arise in your mind. That way, your hunger pangs will be at bay for a significant portion of the fasting period. Moreover, when you complete the first day of your fasting regimen successfully, you will be motivated to make a success of all the days thereafter.

Be active during the fasting window – One of the biggest causes of excessive eating is boredom and the 'nothing to do' feeling. Therefore, make sure you have something productive to do and keep your mind occupied during the fasting period. This way, you will not feel hunger pangs, and also will be distracted enough not to worry about food. Moreover, finding an activity you love doing will enhance the joy of fasting, and your mind is occupied productively elsewhere.

Combine fasting with low-intensity physical activity – Mild exercises and low-intensity physical activity combine extremely well with intermittent fasting and increase lipolysis or fat burning in your body resulting in more weight loss than without exercises. If you lie around lethargically saying that you are fasting, then making a success of your intermittent fasting endeavor is going to be difficult and challenging. Exercises increase endorphin levels too thereby increasing your happiness quotient, which, in turn, could help you manage hunger pangs better.

Drink coffee guilt-free – If you have adopted the 'skipping breakfast' method, then don't forget to get your cup of coffee (sugar-free, of course) before you set out for the day. Drink more cups of tea and coffee right through the fasting period. Caffeine not only takes the edge off your hunger pangs but also boosts lipolysis thereby increasing fat-burning. Remember no sugar, no cream! One word of caution here; avoid drinking so much coffee that you get addicted to it.

Get sufficient sleep – Sufficient sleep is not just a great friend for everyone but also helps in managing your fasting period efficiently. For example, in the 16:8 method, if your fasting period starts at 8 p.m. after a satiating dinner, and your bedtime is 10 p.m., then a significant part of your fasting period is covered in your sleep. You cannot feel hungry when you are asleep!

Additionally, if for some reason you know you are going to be sleep-deprived; perhaps, working on an important project that is due the next day or any other reason, do not indulge in fasting that day. The stress of the lack of sleep will not make the fasting period more stressful than needed.

Take baby steps – Don't take in the plunge straight into the 18:6 or 20:4 method of intermittent fasting. You will fail even before completing an hour of the fasting period. To an untrained mind, the mere thought of fasting for such a long time can result in undue stress. Therefore, start slow.

Initially, skip breakfast for about 2-3 days a week. Increase the number of such days slowly until you are able to skip breakfast on all 7 days of the week. Then, gradually increase the duration of your fasting period by an hour, and keep increasing until you reach your ideal intermittent fasting method.

First, try only for a couple of days – Give yourself a short test period of not more than 2-3 days. Make it a success for this test period, and you will see that you are hooked for life. It is one of the easiest and most efficient ways of gaining health and losing weight.

Treat IF as a form of learning and not some kind of hurdle to cross – If you treat IF as a hurdle, then the stress of winning and losing will enhance the stress of a new lifestyle. Therefore, don't treat it as a hurdle or a test. Simply look at it as a learning experience the outcome of which is only to learn; there is no win or loss.

For example, don't say this, "I will try intermittent fasting for a couple of days, and if it doesn't work then, I will know I have failed." Instead, tell yourself, "I will try intermittent fasting for a couple of days, see how I feel about it, make notes about my experiences, and take it forward from there."

So, get the right mindset to start off on your journey of intermittent fasting, and work hard to be able to leverage its multiple benefits.

What to Expect in the Initial Days and How to Manage the Issues?

It would be naïve to think that intermittent fasting is going to work like a breeze from Day 1. Your body is suddenly undergoing new and unexpected experiences, and it is thrown off-guard for a while. During this time, your body is going to send you signals of discomfort. You must identify these signals and be able to discern as genuine or only initial problems that will pass with time as your body gets accustomed to the new eating pattern. Here are some classic mental and physical reactions that you could encounter along with some tips on how to manage them:

Hunger Pangs

This is, perhaps, the first and the most prominent experience that you will feel during the initial days of your intermittent fasting journey. The ghrelin hormone is responsible for the hunger pangs. Until now, your body is accustomed to getting food every 3-4 hours. Ghrelin levels peak before mealtimes, and when you eat, the level of ghrelin is reduced.

Now that your body will not get the food, ghrelin levels will continue to peak and drive you into deep levels of hunger pangs with each passing minute. It takes a lot of willpower to counter the effects of hunger. However, your body needs only a couple of days to get used to reduced intake of food and the consequent effect of ghrelin to wear off. Here are some tips to manage hunger pangs:

Include a lot of fiber-rich foods in your meal – Fiber-rich foods are known to reduce appetite. Therefore, ensure your meals have a lot of fiber in the form of raw fruit and vegetables, whole grains, beans and legumes, etc. Fiber-rich foods also have a higher water content helping you to remain full for a long time.

Include soups in your meals – Not only do soups make you feel full resulting in less eating during the rest of the meal but they also give you the required amount of micronutrients from the underlying vegetables and/or meat. Of course, it is important to avoid cream-based and high-fat soups. Consume low-calorie and high-fiber soups such as minestrone or bean soups.

Include salads in your meals – Studies have shown that people who eat low-calorie raw salads before a meal eat less during the meal. A simple crunchy salad of celery, carrots, lettuce, tomatoes, and cucumbers with a dash of salt and pepper is yum, filling, and adds very little calories. The fiber in the vegetables enhances your feeling of fullness too.

Your meals must have foods with all three macronutrients included – Don't leave out any of the macronutrients including carbs, proteins, and fats. Your body will crave for a nutrient that is in less supply leaving you feeling hungry sooner than you would like. Just ensure that every macronutrient is in moderate quantities.

Include a portion of grapefruit and/or oranges in your meals or salads – Research studies have shown that grapefruit and oranges have the highest amount of fiber in the fruit and vegetable family, and help to maintain satiety for a sustained period of time helping you manage your hunger pangs effectively.

Drink plenty of water – Staying hydrated helps you manage hunger pangs. In fact, during the initial days of IF when you are acutely aware of hunger pangs, and you consciously make efforts not to eat and instead choose to drink water, you will notice that often hunger is just a reflection of thirst of boredom.

Be active – Just because you are fasting, you must not reduce your normal activity. You could cut down on high-intensity workout sessions during fasting days.

However, continue doing your normal work. The trick with intermittent fasting (until your body gets used to the new eating pattern) is that you must keep your mind occupied and away from thoughts of food. Being active is an effective way to stay focused on things other than food.

Drink calorie-free coffee and tea – Caffeine is an excellent appetite crusher. So include a lot of coffee and tea during your fasting period. Remember to keep it sugar-free and cream-free. A bit of low-fat milk is fine.

And finally, remember feeling hungry is just a natural reminder by your body that it is time for the next meal. Hunger pangs do not translate to muscle loss, death, or anything drastic. Teach your mind to calm down, and choose one or more of the above practical solutions to manage this temporary discomfort.

Cravings

Have you ever told yourself that you will never eat an apple ever again only to reach out for a slice of it in about half an hour? That is how the human mind works. The minute you tell yourself that you will not do something, your mind is so focused on that thing, that you will be compelled to do exactly that thing you didn't want to. Be wary of this feeling when it comes to intermittent fasting.

IF calls for staying away from food, and your mind is invariably going to wander towards food. Specifically, you'll find yourself craving for sweets and refined and processed foods because your mind can easily recall the amazing taste of these foods, and your body wants that glucose hit. Here are some tips to manage cravings:

Drink water – Whenever the craving hits you, drink a glass of water because quite often, cravings are nothing but a reflection of thirst.

Include extra protein in your meals – Proteins reduce cravings and make you full and satiated for a long period of time.

Distract yourself from the craving – Go for a brisk walk or take a shower or do something that you like which will take your mind off the craving. You can also try chewing sugar-free gum.

Plan your meals in advance – When you plan your meals, you avoid spontaneity and the associated concerns regarding what you will eat for your meal. This will reduce temptations and cravings because you will have taken care to include an item you like in your next meal, and that thought will help you manage the desire.

Headaches

Headaches are another common symptom experienced during the early days of intermittent fasting. The causes of these temporary headaches could be lowered blood-sugar levels and stress hormones that are common physiological symptoms of intermittent fasting. With practice, your body will get used to this new routine, and headaches will disappear sooner than later.

Again, keeping yourself hydrated is a good way of preventing headaches while fasting. Ensure you are drinking sufficient amounts of calorie-free liquids in your fasting and feeding windows. Here are some more ways you can manage your stress without medication:

Get yourself a cup of coffee – Caffeine is a great stress-buster and can potentially reduce your headache.

Avoid chewing gum – Chewing gum hurts your jaw and your head. When you have a headache, don't chew gum.

Dim the lights – Whether it is the overhead light or the light from your electronic devices including computers, mobiles, etc. Dim the lights to reduce stress on your eyes.

Practice relaxation techniques – Meditate or do some yoga postures when you have a headache. Chances of pain reduction are very high with these kinds of relaxation techniques.

Low Energy Levels

Mind you, low energy levels are experienced only in the beginning stages. Once your body gets used to fat-burning, you will get an increased boost of energy right through the day. After all, one gram of glucose gives you only 4 calories and one gram of fat gives you 9 calories!

However, before your body becomes an efficient fat-burning machine, the lack of glucose due to fasting will result in lowered energy levels. Here are some tips to manage these initial few days:

Avoid excessive physical activity including high-intensity training and workouts

Keep your days as relaxed as possible

Get some extra sleep

At this juncture, it makes sense to give one more pertinent tip about IF. Don't start your intermittent fasting journey when you are in the middle of an important project at home or at your workplace. The IF routine is going to take some time to get habituated in your head, and therefore, needs the full attention of your body and mind in the initial days. Starting IF in the middle of something important will result in diluted results driving you to wrong conclusions such that IF is not for you.

Irritability

Anger due to hunger is a real phenomenon, and if you have a serious problem with it, then avoiding the IF way is best. However, if you can manage hangry (angry because you are hungry) situations until your body gets accustomed to the new routine, then go ahead, and expect this temporary side-effect to impact your life, and challenge it head-on. Here are some tips:

Avoid situations that enhance stress during this time including people who are habitual annoyers.

Focus on activities that make you happy and joyful so that you feel less irritable

Expect it, and steel your body and mind to be patient for a while

Constipation, Heartburn, and Bloating

Your body is used to releasing digestive enzymes, acids, and hormones during mealtimes. Now, even when the supply of food is not there, these digestive enzymes continue to be released resulting in bloating, heartburn and constipation. These temporary discomforts will continue for a little while until your body gets used to the new eating pattern. The discomfort could range from mild to continuous painful burping. Here are some tips to manage these uncomfortable situations:

Avoid eating greasy and spicy foods during your feeding time

Drink plenty of water

Include a lot of fiber-rich foods to avoid constipation

Prop yourself up when you sleep

If these discomforts don't disappear, then contact your physician.

Feeling Cold

Feeling cold is a good sign of intermittent fasting. The reason for this cold feeling is that when you fast, there is increased blood flow to fat reserves in your body. The increased blood flow facilitates the movement of fat to muscles where it can be processed for energy release. Also, reduced blood sugar levels also result in a feeling of coldness. Here are some tips to manage this feeling of cold:

Sip hot tea

Take warm showers

Wear extra layers of clothing

Don't go out into the cold for long

Overeating

Yes, this is a definite side-effect, especially during the first few days. The reason for overeating during the feeding window could be many including:

A misconceived notion that it is alright to eat whatever you want and how much ever you want during the feeding time

Happiness at completing the fasting without eating a morsel of food can result in forgetting to keep control of food consumption when the fasting period is over

Overexcitement about eating during the feeding time

A sense of dread that hunger pangs will hit you again during the next fasting period, and therefore, it is best to stuff yourself with extra food

Overeating during the feeding time results in weight gain making you think that IF is ineffective. It is important to keep your portions and food consumption normal during feeding time. You must eat as if you are not fasting. Only then will IF work the way it is explained in this book.

Be mindful of your first meal after the fasting period. Plan your meals in advance. In fact, prepare them, and put them into boxes so that you can simply take out the food and eat. There is no need to think much, which can be quite a strain after the fasting period. The strain of thinking of what to eat after the fasting period is bound to make you simply reach out to a couple of slices of pizza and/or a plate of fries with hamburger! Therefore, planning and prepping your feeding time meals in advance is the best way to avoid overeating.

Increased Trips to the Bathroom

You will be drinking large quantities of water to keep yourself hydrated right through the day including your fasting and feeding times. This situation is naturally going to increase your trips to the bathroom. However, there is no way around this except to make the trip whenever nature calls. Do not reduce the intake of water to reduce your bathroom trips.

And finally, always listen to your body and follow its needs. The side-effects mentioned above typically last for a period of 1 to 3 weeks. If any of these side-effects beyond this time or you feel unusually comfortable, stop intermittent fasting.

How to Ease Yourself into Intermittent Fasting

Many of the side-effects of IF cannot be really avoided. They can only be managed. The most effective way of getting into your IF journey is to slowly ease yourself into it. Instead of going from 6 meals a day to 2 meals a day on your first attempt, you must take baby steps, and gradually increase the intensity and duration of the fasting period. Here are some tips to help you with that:

Day 1 – Nothing after dinner

On the first day, do not eat after dinner. Eat all your meals right through the day, but do not eat anything after your dinner. It is quite unlikely that you are hungry after your dinner at 7. However, it is not uncommon for you to snack on popcorn or chips or a cup of ice-cream after dinner as you relax in front of the TV alone or with your family. Avoid this on Day 1. If you are used to this, then getting through the night on Day 1 without that snack might be challenging. Here are some helpful tips:

Replace popcorn/chips/ice-cream with warm herbal tea or plain water.

Brush your teeth immediately after your dinner. Not only does the minty taste of toothpaste help in curbing cravings, but your subconscious mind also gets a signal that you are done eating for the day which, in turn, helps turn off the activity of ghrelin hormone.

Go straight to bed.

Day 2 – Delayed breakfast

Even if you are an early bird and wake up at 6 a.m., you will have finished 11 hours of fasting. If you wake up at around 7 a.m., which is typical for most people, then you will be 12 hours into your fasting period. So, persist a little more and delay your breakfast.

Anyway, you may be in a rush to get ready for the office, and busy with all your other activities. So, have a cup of coffee, pack a light breakfast (maybe sandwiches made with whole grain bread), and eat it along with your morning coffee in the office at 10 a.m. that's it. You will have already completed about 14 hours of fasting time. Here's what your day will look like:

10 a.m. – breakfast

12 noon – it may be lunchtime, but it is quite likely that you are not hungry because of the delayed breakfast; so, feel free to push your lunchtime to 2 p.m.

2 p.m. – lunch

5 p.m. – a little snack

7 p. m. – dinner, and nothing more; just like Day 1

Day 3 – Avoid the evening snack

Continue the same food timetable as Day 1 and Day 2 except remove the evening snack. Here are some tips to help you overcome the snack craving:

Remind yourself that your dinner is only a couple of hours away, and you are really not very hungry right now. It is only a habit that is being triggered.

Have a cup of sugar-free coffee, tea, or lemonade.

Stay active and indulge in some activity until dinnertime so that you don't focus on your craving, which is temporary and will go away if you don't respond to it.

Day 4 – Delay breakfast by another hour

So, instead of breakfast at 10 a.m. have your breakfast at 11 a.m. Then, you will be able to delay your lunch to 3 p.m., and your dinner at 7 p.m. that's it. You have managed to achieve the 16:8 method of intermittent fasting within four days of slowly easing your body and mind into the process.

Nearly all the therapeutic effects of intermittent fasting will kick in with this 16:8 method also referred to as the Leangains method. When you are thoroughly fixed into this regimen with absolutely no sign of any side-effects whatsoever, try and extend your intermittent fasting to the more rigorous ones.

For example, moving into the 18:6 method can happen seamlessly after a fortnight of strictly following the 16:8 regimen. Keep to the 18:6 regimen for as long as your body takes to get accustomed to it. When you are fine with it, then you can move on to the 20-hour, the 24-hour, and the alternate day methods, which are more difficult to manage. However, if you are patient with yourself, and take baby steps at each stage, you will notice that not only are you losing weight but also becoming far more energetic than before your IF days.

Chapter Five: Intermittent Fasting and Weight Loss

Weight Loss is one of the most or even the most significant benefits of intermittent fasting. Therefore, it makes sense to dedicate an entire chapter to this crucial element of IF. Before we go into how IF benefits weight loss, you need to correctly understand some of the misconceived aspects of our metabolism.

Important Points to Remember About Our Metabolism

The following points about your metabolism will help you understand how intermittent fasting is most effective for weight loss:

Metabolism takes place in every cell of your body – It is common to hear people talking about human metabolism like it is an organ or a body part, which you can control. In truth, metabolism is nothing but a series of chemical reactions that take place in each cell. The basic metabolic rate (BMR) is the minimum amount of energy (measured in calories) needed for your body functions to take place smoothly when you are at complete rest. It is the total energy needed to keep the different cells, tissues, organs, and organ systems to function normally and without a hitch when you are at rest.

A significant portion (nearly 50%) of your body's basic metabolic rate is used by for the functioning of the major organs including the heart, brain, kidneys and liver. The rest of the BMR is used by the digestive system, the body's muscles, fats, and others.

BMR accounts for the largest amount of calories burned by your body – Your body burns calories in three different ways including:

BMR or the energy needed to continue your body's normal functioning when you are at rest

Thermic effect is the energy required to break down consumed food into energy

The energy needed for the physical activity you do

Studies have revealed that BMR accounts for nearly 60-80% of the energy burned during the day. Breaking down food takes up about 10%. Energy for physical activity uses up only 10-30% although people in high-performance sports could use up a little more.

This observation is especially useful for people who think that if they exercise enough, they can eat what they want and when they want. The truth is that weight loss, of course, requires a combination of reduced intake and increased usage of calories.

Metabolism varies between different people, and there is no scientific explanation for the phenomenon – Two people with similar body weight, size, and composition can have different metabolism, and currently, there is no scientific explanation for this difference. Though some studies seem to connect metabolism to lean mass, fat tissue, age, gender, and perhaps, genetics, there is no conclusive evidence as yet for the anomaly.

Advancing age slows down metabolism – It has been proven that advancing age definitely slows down metabolism. Even if your muscle and fat composition at 60 is the same as it was when you were 20, the BMR will show a decreased figure now. The decline of metabolism is believed to start as early as 18 years.

Slowing metabolism does not prevent you from losing weight and keeping the lost weight off – Multiple experiments have revealed that it is highly possible to lose weight and keep it off even when your metabolism is reducing. The trick is to identify and make positive lifestyle changes that you can adhere to over a sustained period of time, preferably your entire lifetime. Intermittent fasting is definitely one such lifestyle change that is sustainable and positively impacts your long-term weight-loss program without creating undue stress and anxiety that are normally associated with crash diets.

Intermittent Fasting and Weight Loss

You already read about how the body has two sources of energy; one from the consumed food in the form of glucose (fed state), and the other from stored food primarily in the form of fat and some of it in the form of glycogen (fasted state). The crucial point to remember is that your body can access energy from only one of these two sources at a time.

For example, if it is in the fed state, then your body accesses only the energy from the consumed food. And when it is in the fasted state, it can access only the energy from stored fat. The body cannot access energy both from consumed food and stored food simultaneously.

When the body is in the fed state, it is easy to use the glucose coming from the consumed for energy, and that is the default option. During the fed state, insulin levels are high which triggers the fat-burning process or lipolysis and the conversion of stored glycogen to glucose (gluconeogenesis) to shut down.

Typically, when you have not yet started the fasting regimen, and you consume 3-4 meals a day, this is what is happening right through the day; the fat-burning process is completely shut down. Now, in the same situation, let us see what happens when we sleep during which time you don't eat any food. No consumption of food translates to lowered insulin levels, which, in turn, signals the body to start using energy from its stored reserves. That is the reason you wake up instead of dying at night even though you have not eaten for nearly 10-12 hours.

When you voluntary fast during the day, the same thing happens. The insulin level falls, which is the trigger for the body to switch to, stored food for its energy needs. So, first, the body reaches out to the limited supply of stored glycogen in the liver and muscles, and when this is exhausted, it turns to the abundant supply of fat energy from the adipose tissues deposited all over the body.

Suppose your BMR is 2000 calories. This means you need 2000 calories of energy to simply get the basic physiological functions in your body to take place seamlessly. When you fast for 24 hours, this requirement of 2000 calories is taken from the large reserve of fat energy stored in your body. By the way, 2000 calories accounts for about half a pound of fat!

This process of reaching out to stored food for energy is the reason for human survival across millennia. If we didn't have this natural mechanism, we would have been wiped out millions of years ago because food was not always available in plenty to our hunter-gatherer ancestors, and therefore, intermittent fasting is a natural and healthy process for weight loss.

The summary is this: the body either uses fat or stores fat. When food is available in plenty, then it stores fat, and when food is scarce, the body uses fat. The critical regulator of this process is insulin, and therefore, it makes sense to spend some time on this crucial digestive hormone.

The Significance of Insulin in Intermittent Fasting

The differences in the levels of insulin are what triggers the body to switch between consumed food and stored food for its energy. When insulin levels are high, your body uses consumed food for its energy, and when the insulin levels are low, it uses the stored food for energy.

So, when you use traditional ways of diets to lose fat, you are most often compelled to eat about 4-6 times a day resulting in your insulin levels remaining high at all times. This situation ensures your body hardly ever reaches out to the stored food for its energy needs. As insulin is high, your body's energy needs have to come from consumed food as it cannot access stored food during this time.

So, in conventional diets, suppose you restrict your calorie intake from 2000 to 1500 a day. You do this in the hope that you lose weight because your body is consuming less energy than the BMR. However, as you are eating 4-6 times a day insulin levels are always at high levels right through the day. Initially, you do lose weight from these diets.

However, as your body can never access the stored food or fat reserves, it makes adjustments to reduce the

BMR itself to 1500 calories resulting in reduced metabolism. Therefore, after the initial few days (when you do lose weight), with conventional diets, the weight loss plateaus because your metabolism has slowed down to adjust to the new calorie intake.

Not only does your weight loss stop, but reduced metabolism makes you feel exhausted and irritable. And soon, your body weight increases which makes you want to give up the endeavor. So, you increase your calorie intake to 1700 per day, which is still less than 2000 (your initial BMR). However, now you are in a situation wherein your BMR is 1500, and you are consuming 1700 calories resulting in weight gain slowly but surely.

Therefore, the crucial element is weight loss is not only reducing calories but also reducing insulin levels. Insulin is the switch fat storage and fat usage. You want your body to remain primarily in the fat usage stage, and to achieve this, you must reduce insulin levels. The most natural way to reduce insulin levels is to put your body increasingly in a fasted state. That is why, intermittent fasting is the most natural and effective means of fat loss, and consequently, weight loss.

Critical Points to Remember for Effective Weight Loss

Weight loss is primarily caused by fat loss, which happens if we eat fewer calories than we need each day; a phenomenon referred to as 'calorie deficit.' To achieve this calorie deficit, intermittent fasting has to work in conjunction with the following elements:

Quality of food – Avoid unprocessed refined foods completely, and stick to wholesome, wholegrain, and nutritious foods.

Calorie consumption – Making up for the loss of calorie intake during fasting by overeating in the feeding window will not help you lose weight in any way. In fact, you will end up gaining weight even after attempting IF for a sufficiently long time.

Patience – Your body needs time to get used to a new way of living. If you rush through the initial days without giving your body sufficient leeway to get accustomed to the various changes brought on by IF, it is going to get confused which can have disastrous results.

Consistency – IF has to be implemented consistently for effective benefits to be achieved. You cannot expect to do IF for a couple of months and revert back to your old eating pattern. It is a lifestyle change that has to be put in place so that it lasts consistently throughout your life.

Exercise – Fasting does not allow you to lead a sedentary lifestyle. You have to continue to do whatever you did before you started your fasting regimen. Combining exercise and fasting is believed to multiply the fat loss process resulting in more effective fat loss than if the two elements were tried separately.

FAQs on Weight Loss by Intermittent Fasting

Here are some FAQs on how intermittent fasting affects weight loss. Most of your questions will be found here.

How much of weight loss can I expect with intermittent fasting?

Weight loss by intermittent fasting depends on multiple factors including:

The extent of your fasting window

The fasting method you choose

What you consume during the feeding period

However, when you reach a fasting duration of 16-20 hours a day on a consistent basis, then you can potentially lose 2-3 pounds of fat each week. In addition to losing weight, the other 'cool' benefit of intermittent fasting is how it simplifies the meal planning and prep work because you have now reduced your meals from 4-6 a day to 1-3 a day!

Can I continue to exercise when I fast?

Yes, absolutely. You might have to reduce your high-intensity workouts during the initial days when your energy levels are slightly low. This is a short period of time when your body is still learning to burn fat efficiently and your food consumption is also reduced which results in reduced energy levels. During this phase, which usually lasts for a couple of weeks, it might be a good idea not to indulge in high-intensity workouts to conserve energy.

In fact, once your body gets accustomed to burning fat, your energy levels will see an increase, and you will find it easy to remain physically and mentally alert right through the day without signs of fatigue or hunger driving you crazy even on highly active days.

Is Fasting Safe?

Fasting is one of the most natural methods to burn stored fat in the human body and has been in existence since time immemorial. You are not force-feeding your body with anything at all. There are no new elements or ingredients that are being tried in this method. You are only driving your body to access its own stored food, and therefore, intermittent fasting is one of the safest and most natural methods of weight loss.

However, there are certain contraindications such as pregnancy, an underlying medical condition such as diabetes, and more for which you must take care. These aspects have been discussed in detail in Chapter Two.

Chapter Six: Mistakes to Avoid and Other Important Information about Intermittent Fasting

Now that you know a lot of information including various benefits of intermittent fasting, it is time to learn about some of the most common avoidable mistakes that beginners do. This knowledge will help you plan your IF journey well and ensure you achieve success. Here are some easily discernible and avoidable mistakes of novices:

Choosing the Wrong Method of Intermittent Fasting

Chapter Three discusses the different methods of intermittent fasting, and nearly all of them are effective to leverage multiple benefits of IF. It is imperative that you choose a method that is aligned with your personal needs and lifestyle. Do not get carried away by what others are doing. Think objectively and make the right choice.

For example, the 5:2 method calls for reducing your calorie intake to just about 500-600 calories on the fasting days. Now, if you lead an active life with a family and kids, full-time work that is quite stressful, and regular visits to the gym, then this method might not be the best because you will not be able to maintain your active lifestyle on the fasting days with significantly reduced calorie intake.

With this kind of lifestyle, maybe starting off with the simple 12-hour fasting, and gradually increasing it to the 16:8 or the 18:6 method might be the best option. However, you must make this choice on your own. For beginners especially, it is important to start small to prevent feeling disillusioned with failures driven by setting unreasonable expectations.

Moving Excessively Fast in the Intermittent Fasting Journey

If, for example, you are used to 5 meals a day, and you choose to move to the 16:8 or even trying to fast for 10 hours at a stretch during daytime might be counterproductive to success. Your body needs time to adjust itself to the new eating pattern. Start with baby steps, and ensure you don't rush through the journey to reach your peak level of intermittent fasting quickly.

The results of impatience will be disastrous, and you are bound to feel disappointed and dissatisfied. Use the pattern mentioned in Chapter Four to ease yourself into intermittent fasting slowly but surely. This approach will result in sustained success.

The same logic holds good for your exercise regimen during IF. If, for example, you are used to morning workouts, and now, you are starting off your IF regimen by skipping breakfast, you might have to change your workout timings to a more suitable time, at least until your body is set in the new ways.

So, the crucial aspect to remember is to be patient with yourself and your body. It takes time to make changes, especially sustainable positive ones. Don't be overambitious and spoil your chances of success.

Obsessed with Keeping Perfect Time

For example, if your lunch is to be at 12 noon, you don't have to wait for the stroke of twelve to eat. Don't obsess over time. Eat when you are sufficiently close to the end of the fasting period. A few minutes this side or that side is not really going to make a difference to your results.

The problem with this kind of obsession is that it creates undue stress making it easier to give up your efforts. Therefore, don't waste your resources obsessing over micromanaging your intermittent fasting timetable. Just relax and listen to your body and mind.

Giving Up Trying Very Soon

Setting your body into the right rhythm of intermittent fasting takes a lot of effort and a lot of time. The initial few days are the toughest because your body and mind are battling with multiple new mindset and physiological changes. It is natural for your body to resist changes of any kind, and it will create discomforts in various forms (discussed in detail in Chapter Four) to try and dissuade you from the effort.

Acknowledge this natural response of your body, learn about the different ways it will resist, and prepare yourself mentally and physically to manage them. With patience and persistence, you will notice your energy levels slowly rising, your ability to manage hunger pangs increasing, and your body slowly adapting to fat-burning techniques. Until this happens, don't give up on yourself. Success lies on the other side of hard work.

Excessive Eating During Feeding Periods

Until you recognize the correct balance between eating and overeating, you must err on the side of caution, and eat less than you planned. This approach is important to ensure you don't overeat during your feeding window.

Initially, you will feel so famished after a fasting period that you could easily end up eating more than you need defeating the very purpose of fasting to reduce calorie intake. Be wary of this mistake, and eat your meals mindfully to prevent overeating. Use the tips and tricks given in Chapter Four on how to prevent overeating.

Eating Very Little During Feeding Periods

As you get deeper into your fasting regimen, you will need increasingly smaller quantities of food to fill satiated. You don't feel very hungry after some time into, and many times, it is possible that you forget that your fasting period is over, and you need to eat!

It is important not to under-eat as well because the lack of sufficient nutrients could potentially lead to other health issues. Additionally, your focus and your attention span could be affected preventing you from reaching your peak performance levels. Therefore, ensure you never dip below the 1200 calorie mark on an average every week.

Eating the Wrong Kinds of Foods

Intermittent fasting is not as strict as other diets when it comes to eating what you want. However, it is not a free-for-all niche too. You cannot eat pizzas, fries, and burgers for every meal. It is critical that you nourish your body with all three macronutrients in well-balanced meals.

This balanced approach will not only keep you satiated for a sustained period of time but also allow your body to be nourished in a healthy way. Your brain, your muscle, and all other organs will develop healthily when macronutrients are available in sufficient quantities.

Not Being Active

Fasting can make you very restless because your mind is already quite stressed out about going hungry. If you cannot find ways to distract your mind and body, breaking the fast (even when you are not hungry) will be the first and only thing that captures your attention. Therefore, don't stop your normal activities when you start off your IF journey. Live as you normally do. Only follow the eating pattern as described in this book.

Overusing Caffeine

When you skip breakfast, drinking one or two cups of coffee is the most natural response to stave off hunger. However, overuse of caffeine can be disastrous because if you don't stop yourself with a couple of cups, you are going to get addicted to caffeine, and with any addiction, the purpose of the original intermittent fasting journey will be forgotten.

Best Foods for Intermittent Fasting

Water – Whether you are in the fasting or feasting window, the importance of being can never be overstated. Water is the most important element in each and every cell of the body. It is imperative that no cell of your body dies due to the lack of water. Hydration helps to overcome negative side-effects such as headaches, hunger pangs, and more.

The amount of water needed varies for each individual. The sign of your body being well-hydrated is that your urine should be a pale yellow color. Dark yellow urine reveals your body is not hydrated enough. Dehydration causes headaches, lightheadedness, and fatigue.

If you combine lack of water with fasting, then disaster is sure to strike. So, avoid this situation by drinking plenty of water. If you find water plain and boring, add a dash of lime, soak some slices of cucumber, and add a couple of sprigs of mint to boost the taste and texture of water. You will love this.

Fish – Fish is a rich source of proteins and healthy fats. Fish is also very rich in Vitamin D that is crucial for calcium absorption. Moreover, if you are limited food intake, then fish referred to as 'brain food' can be an excellent supplement for improved functioning of the brain. Make sure you include fish in your meals.

Avocado – The high concentration of healthy monosaturated fats in avocado ensures you remain satiated for a sustained period of time. Multiple studies have revealed that eating even half an avocado can stave off hunger pangs for long hours.

Cruciferous vegetables – The cruciferous vegetable family consists of cauliflower, cabbage, broccoli, and Brussel sprouts. These veggies are full of fiber; an unmissable element for the success of intermittent fasting. Moreover, these veggies help to keep constipation and other digestive tract-related disorders at bay. Fiber-rich foods also keep you satiated for a long time preventing the onset of painful hunger pangs.

Beans and legumes – Black beans, chickpeas, lentils, and peas are excellent sources of low-carb proteins allowing you to get both these macronutrients in balanced quantities. In fact, these listed beans and legumes are known to decrease body weight even without reducing calorie intake.

Potatoes – We are not talking potato fries that come with hamburgers or chips that come with fish chips. We are talking about well-cooked potatoes because the carbs in this vegetable are known to be one of the most satiating carbs in the world. Baked potatoes with skin on, and other such healthy and oil-free potatoes dishes are great additions to your meals.

Probiotics – Your gut's flora and fauna are responsible for a healthy digestive process. When your stomach is empty, then these gut flora and fauna can create unpleasant side-effects such as constipation. Probiotic-rich foods such as sauerkraut, kombucha, and kefir are excellent to counter these negative effects.

Eggs – Eggs are complete meals by themselves, and are so easy to cook. The protein-rich food is excellent to keep your hunger-free for a long period of time. Studies have shown that people who ate an egg in the morning felt far less hungry than people who did not consume eggs.

Berries – Strawberries, blueberries, and other members of the berry family are rich in Vitamin C; an essential micronutrient for the health of your immune system. Additionally, some studies have revealed that eating flavonoid-rich berries in the long term can reduce your BMI.

Nuts – While nuts have a big calorific value as compared to raw fruit and vegetables, they contain polyunsaturated fat, which is considered 'good fat.' A few nuts to snack on will take care of your fat needs for the day. In fact, walnuts are believed to change certain physiological markers that affect appetite and satiety.

Whole grains – Whole grains might be all carbs on the face of it. However, they are rich in proteins as well as fibers and keep you feeling full and hunger-free for a sustained period of time. Studies have also revealed that eating whole grains instead of refined foods can potentially increase your metabolism. Therefore, make sure you include bulgur wheat, amaranth, kamut, sorghum, millets, and other such cereals in some of your meals.

Foods to Avoid During Intermittent Fasting

Sugar – You must avoid sugars of all kinds including honey, artificial sweeteners, etc. Drinking sweetened tea or coffee is like eating a fistful of candies resulting in the spiking of insulin levels almost immediately. When insulin is released, the effectiveness of your intermittent fasting is lost. Studies have revealed that even commercially available zero-calorie artificial sweeteners trigger the release of insulin. Therefore, it is best to completely avoid sugars during intermittent fasting.

Foods with hidden calories – Multiple foods in the market call themselves sugar-free but sneak in some calories in a couple of ingredients. For example, clear broth, bottled water, etc. could have ingredients with calorific values that could negatively impact the effectiveness of intermittent fasting. Be cautious about these items, and read the label, and ensure it is truly zero-calorie product before consuming.

Refined foods – All kinds of processed and refined foods are to be avoided because they trigger the highest levels of insulin release.

Conclusion

Intermittent fasting is not some kind of new diet that has been introduced to the world in the recent past. It is as old as humankind. Starting from our hunter-gatherer ancestors who fasted from compulsion and food shortage to the wise men in nearly all ancient civilizations to religions, fasting was a way of healing, resting the body, and an act of self-control and penitence.

Modern science is only ratifying what our ancestors already knew and implemented without a doubt. Intermittent fasting is, therefore, nothing but a new name given to an age-old custom that got lost somewhere in the depths of development, wealth, and progress. It makes sense to complete this book by summarizing the amazing benefits of intermittent fasting so that you feel motivated to implement in your life.

Shifts our metabolism from glucose to fat – Our metabolic fire has to burn continuously as long as we are alive. The fuel for this fire comes either from consumed food or stored food. The unfortunate aspect of modern life is that many of us have stored food in excess of our needs. Intermittent fasting triggers the body to reach out to the stored food for its fuel so that it is used up and we are left with the right balance of stored food and consumed food in our systems. Effectively, IF triggers fat metabolism resulting in all the benefits listed below.

Reduces fat content all over the body including stubborn belly fat – When the body goes into fat metabolism, it uses fat sources from all over the body including from the belly area which consists of stubborn fat (referred to as visceral fat) that is the most difficult to burn. So, you can easily get a flat stomach if you persist in your IF efforts.

Increases energy levels – Fat metabolism results in more energy being released than carb metabolism. Therefore, after the initial few days during which time your body is learning to become an efficient fat-burning machine, you will feel more energetic than before with improved productivity.

Reduced inflammation and oxidative stress – Intermittent fasting results in reduced inflammation and oxidative stress which, in turn, benefits your body in many ways including:

Slows down aging

Fights against multiple health disorders caused by inflammation and oxidative stress

Improves skin texture and smoothness

Frees up energy for more productive work – Intermittent fasting is the most natural way of resting your digestive system that needs to work almost without a break. The body's focus is shifted from digesting food to other important work such as cell repair and maintenance, clearing of toxic wastes from the body, and more.

Intermittent fasting is not some kind of crash diet. It is a life-changing habit that is expected to last a lifetime and brings with it a host of benefits that has immensely positive impact on your life. It would be naïve not to try this method of losing weight and leading a healthier life than before. You would be doing a disservice to yourself if you didn't try intermittent fasting and leverage its multiple benefits simply because of fears and biases. So, go ahead, reread the book, make sure you have understood how IF works, and plunge right in.

Book 2

Ketogenic Miracle

Enhancing Health while Increasing Weight Loss Success

How can you avoid Ketogenic Diet mistakes

By:Emily Simmons

Introduction

Folks, you have this amazing book called Ketogenic Diet Mistakes You Need to Know in your hands. You must have already read a lot about the Ketogenic Diet before starting it. Of course, it is always easy to start something, but a lot more difficult to stick to it. This doesn't only apply to difficult things. Many people struggle to see even a small commitment through to the end.

A lot more than determination and willpower are needed to stay committed to the Ketogenic Diet. This book deals with the requirements and hazards of the Ketogenic Diet in full detail. Go through the chapters given in this book. You will not find any dearth of knowledge about this "intimidating" diet. You will hopefully feel more enlightened after reading this book, because it sheds enough light on the concept to chase away all your feelings of intimidation.

Before just jumping into the area that deals with common mistakes, we have given you some general information on the Ketogenic Diet- the foods you should and shouldn't eat, things you must and must not do, and the possible mistakes that you need to learn to watch out for. It is smarter to learn from the mistakes of others. It saves you much time, energy, and money. Otherwise, when you do not take the precautionary steps and keep making the mistakes, you'll quickly start to feel miserable and will most likely quit the regime.

You have made a smart move by starting with this book. This proves that you are willing to improve your well-being. We have very fast lives these days and it is always better to be prepared beforehand rather than repent later. If you have already started the Ketogenic regime, you still have enough time to learn the hazards in case you have been unintentionally causing trouble for yourself. If you have not yet started it, please take the time to read this Bible of the Ketogenic Diet and only then take your first step. We'll lay any lingering anxieties you may have to rest. Why not invite a few friends along on this health-filled journey and ask them to support you if they are willing? It's always easier to complete the course when you have someone along with you.

Just set aside your inhibitions and let's get started.

Remember to enjoy the journey rather than only look at the target.

Our best wishes are with you!

Chapter 1

What is the Ketogenic Diet?

The Ketogenic Diet, also known as Keto Diet, is based on the concept of eating fewer carbohydrates and more fats. This makes the body produce ketones in the liver that are used as energy. You must be wondering what ketones are. Well, they are the acids or organic compounds which are produced when our bodies start using fats for energy in place of carbohydrates. When our bodies do not have enough glucose obtained from sugar in the blood to transport it into the cells, our bodies use fats instead and break them down to supply us with energy. However, high levels of ketones are harmful for the body, and may lead to a condition called ketoacidosis.

The Ketogenic Diet has been in existence for more than 5 decades, but has risen in popularity in the last few years. It is famously known by many names: Low Carbs Diet, LCHF (Low Carb High Fat Diet), Keto Diet, etc.

When our diets are rich in carbohydrates, our body produces insulin and glucose.

It is easiest for the body to make energy from glucose. Thus, it automatically chooses glucose over any other molecule to convert it into energy. Insulin performs the activity of taking glucose around your body and processes it in your bloodstream. Now, you can understand that since glucose is mainly used as a primary source of energy, fats are not usually used and therefore they are stored in different parts of our bodies. This makes our bodies bulky.

Our normal diet is high in carbohydrates, which provides glucose as the primary source of energy. When we lower the intake of carbohydrates, the body is encouraged to enter into a condition called ketosis. It is a natural process, which is initiated by the body when we consume less food. During this condition, our body produces ketones by breaking down fats taken from the liver.

The primary goal of a well maintained ketogenic diet is to encourage our bodies to enter this state of metabolism. This does not mean that we have to starve for calories, but we do need to cut down on carbohydrates. This has a plus side to it. We can indulge in a lot of fats and still not feel guilty about it. However, we need to look out for some common mistakes, which we will talk about later.

Our bodies are made to be extremely adaptive. We can put them through whatever conditions we have to and they can adjust. Even when we snatch a major portion of carbohydrates from our diet, we will not feel weak once our bodies adapt to the new diet. They will start utilizing ketones as the primary source of energy.

Chapter 2

What should you eat?

If you want to begin the Ketogenic Diet, you will need to plan very well because this diet does not suit everyone. You must have a practicable diet plan before you begin. Whatever you consume depends on how quickly you want to enter into the state of ketosis. The faster you quit carbohydrates, the quicker you will reach ketosis.

Normally, the net amount of carbs specified for the Keto Diet is 20-30 grams every day. You might be wondering, "What are net carbs?" Don't worry. It's really simple. "Net carbs" means the total carbs in your diet minus the amount of fiber. For example, 100 grams of lettuce contains 3 grams of carbohydrates and 1.3 grams of dietary fiber. So, we can deduce that if we subtract 1.3 grams of fiber from 3 grams of carbohydrates, we are left with 1.7 grams of net carbs.

It may be a challenge to stick to a healthy diet low on carbs, particularly when you have just started it. However, owing to the popularity of this diet nowadays, you will not find any shortage of recipes to look for which contain fewer carbohydrates. You can go through the list below of foods friendly to the Keto Diet to help you make the appropriate choices. You must keep one thing in mind: that you have to eat real food, not only food that is low in carbohydrates. Foods like eggs, meats, nuts, vegetables, yoghurt, and some fruits occasionally. Also, you must avoid any kind of processed food which may contain colorings and preservatives.

Following the Ketogenic Diet does not mean that you have to lose weight regardless of the cost. It is all about taking on a healthier lifestyle.

You can eat these things freely:

Wild animals and grass fed animal sources of protein

Grass fed meat simply means that it is the meat of an animal which grazes grass. You can indulge in the grass fed meat of goat, lamb, beef, and venison.

Wild caught seafood and fish, pastured poultry and pork, ghee, gelatin, pastured eggs, and butter. These foods have a high content of omega 3 fatty acids.

You must keep away from farmed fish, meat and sausages covered with breadcrumbs, meat which comes with starchy or sugary sauces, and hot dogs.

You can also eat the offal (heart, liver, kidneys, and meat of other organs) of grass fed animals.

Healthy fats

Saturated fats like tallow, lard, goose fat, duck fat, clarified butter or ghee, coconut oil, butter.

Monounsaturated fat like macadamia, avocado, olive oil.

Polyunsaturated omega 3's, from animal sources like seafood and fatty fish.

Non-starchy vegetables

Cruciferous vegetables like kohlrabi, kale, and radish leaves.

Leafy greens like bok choy, Swiss chard, lettuce, spinach, endive, chives, radicchio, etc.

Celery stalks, cucumber, asparagus, summer squash (spaghetti squash, zucchini), bamboo shoots.

Condiments and beverages

Coffee (with coconut cream or black coffee), still water, black or herbal tea.

Pork rinds for breading.

Mustard, mayonnaise, homemade bone broth, pesto, pickles, homemade fermented foods like kombucha, kimchi, sauerkraut, etc.

All herbs and spices, lime or lemon zest and juice.

Whey protein, egg white protein, grass fed and hormone free gelatin. Keep away from artificial sweeteners, additives, soy lecithin, hormones.

Fruits

Avocado

You can eat these foods occasionally:

Fruits, vegetables and mushrooms

Cruciferous vegetables like green and white cabbage, cauliflower, red cabbage, broccoli, fennel, Brussels sprouts, turnips, swede/ rutabaga.

Nightshades (eggplant, peppers, tomatoes).

Root vegetables like parsley root, leek, spring onion, onion, mushrooms, garlic, winter squash like pumpkin.

Sea vegetables like kombu, and nori; okra, bean sprouts, wax beans, sugar snap peas, water chestnuts, globe or French artichokes.

Berries (blueberries, blackberries, strawberries, cranberries, raspberries, mulberries, etc.)

Coconut, rhubarb, olives.

Full-fat dairy and grain-fed animals

Beef, eggs, poultry, and ghee (stay away from farmed pork, as it has high content of omega 6's!)

Dairy products (cottage cheese, full-fat yogurt, sour cream, cream, cheese.)

Stay away from products which are labeled "low-fat". Many of these products are packed with starch and sugar. They do not have any satiating effect.

Bacon. Be cautious of added starches and preservatives. You can consume nitrates if you have antioxidants in your diet.

Seeds and nuts

Macadamia nuts which are low in carbs and high in omega 3's.

Almonds, pecans, walnuts, pine nuts, hazelnuts, flaxseed, sesame seeds, sunflower seeds, hemp seeds, pumpkin seeds.

Brazil nuts (be cautious of their high selenium content, and eat only very small amount of them.

Soy products (fermented)

If you eat any soy products, eat only fermented or non GMO soy products like tempeh, natto, soy sauce or coconut aminos (paleo-friendly).

Green soy beans or edamame, unprocessed black soy beans.

Condiments

Zero carbohydrate healthy sweeteners (Swerve, Stevia, Erythritol, etc.)

Tomato products (sugar free) like passata, puree, ketchup.

Thickeners like xanthan gum, and arrowroot powder. Remember that xanthan gum is not a paleo friendly gum; still it is used by many paleo followers since you need only a small amount of it.

Extra dark chocolate (it is better to take 70% or 90% chocolate, do not take any soy lecithin), carob and cocoa powder.

Do not take mints and chewing gums. Some of them contain carbohydrates.

Some fruits, vegetables, seeds and nuts with limited carbohydrates- depending on your daily limit of carbohydrates

Root vegetables (carrot, celery root, beetroot, sweet potato, and parsnip)

Watermelon Cantaloupe / Honeydew melons/ Galia

Cashew and pistachio nuts, chestnuts

Very small amounts of dragon fruits, apricots, peaches, apples, nectarines, grapefruits, kiwi berries, kiwifruit, oranges, cherries, plums, figs (fresh), pears

Alcohol

You can drink dry white wine, dry red wine, or unsweetened spirits. However, if you are on a weight loss regime, it is best to avoid them. These drinks should only be taken once you reach the weight maintenance stage.

You must avoid these foods:

It is important to avoid food containing a high content of carbohydrates, processed foods and factory farmed meat.

All kinds of grains and artificial sweets

Avoid whole grains such as wheat, oats, corn, rye, barley, bulgur, sorghum, millet, rice, amaranth, sprouted grains, and buckwheat. This automatically encompasses products made of grains like pasta, pizza, bread, crackers, cookies, etc.

Avoid white potatoes and quinoa

Avoid sugar, sweets, etc. like table sugar, agave syrup, HFCS, ice-creams, sweet puddings, cakes, and sugary soft-drinks

Fish and pork farmed in factories

They have high content of omega 6 fatty acids which causes inflammation in the body. Farmed fish also contains PCBs. You must also avoid fish with a high mercury content.

Artificial sweeteners

Splenda, sweeteners containing Aspartame, Equal, Acesulfame, Saccharin, Sucralose, etc.

Processed foods

Processed foods which contain carrageenan

MSG (it is contained in a few whey protein products

Sulphites in gelatin and dried fruits

BPAs, they are not always labeled

Wheat gluten

Refined oils and fats

Sunflower, safflower, canola, cottonseed, soybean, corn oil, grapeseed

Trans-fats such as margarine

Products labeled low fat, low carbs, zero carbs

Atkins products, diet drinks and soda

Chewing mints and gums may contain a high content of carbs, or they may also contain gluten, artificial additives, etc.

Milk

A very small amount of full fat raw milk is permissible on the Ketogenic Diet.

Other than that, milk is prohibited for many reasons. Among all dairy products, milk is the most difficult one to digest because it contains few good bacteria. (They are destroyed during pasteurization.) Milk may also contain hormones.

Also, milk is high in carbohydrates. There are almost 4-5 grams of carbs in 100 milliliters of milk.

If you want to make tea or coffee, you can put cream in measured amounts.

Though you can drink small quantities of milk, you must make a note of the total carbohydrates.

Sweet drinks and alcohol

Sweet wine, beer, and cocktails must be avoided.

Tropical fruits

Mango, pineapple, papaya, and banana should be avoided.

Fruits high in carbs should also be avoided such as grapes, tangerines, etc.

You must also avoid fruit juices (both packed and fresh). However, you may drink smoothies in limited quantities. Juices are like water with sugar, but smoothies contain fiber, and they are more satiating.

You must also avoid large quantities of dried fruits like raisins and dates. You may consume them in moderate quantities.

Soy products

You must avoid most of the soy products, excluding non-GMO fermented products that are good for health.

Other things to keep away from

You must keep away from wheat gluten which is present in low-carbs foods. You will have to give up bread.

Stay away from cans lined with BPA. If possible, you must look for BPA-free containers like glass jars. BPA is partly responsible for many health ailments like impaired thyroid function, cancer, etc.

[BPA implies bisphenol A. It is a chemical used in industries which make a particular kind of resins and plastics. It is normally found in epoxy resins and polycarbonate plastics. Such plastics are used to make containers that store beverages and food. Epoxy resins are applied on the inside of containers like food cans, water supply lines and bottle tops.

Research has shown that BPA is capable of seeping into beverages and foods from these containers, which is terrible for health. Thus, it is better to avoid products packed in such containers.]

You must avoid other additives like carrageenan, MSG, sulfites.

Chapter 3

What Can You Expect From the Ketogenic Diet?

Benefits of following the Ketogenic Diet:

What benefits do you get from following such a strict diet? There are many. Not only does the Ketogenic Diet help you to lose weight, but it also gives you the following advantages:

Cholesterol: The Ketogenic Diet improves your cholesterol and triglyceride levels, which are mostly linked with the clogging up of arteries.

Weight loss: Since your body burns fat for energy in this diet, your body weight automatically comes down during the state of fasting.

Blood sugar: LDL cholesterol decreases over time with the Keto diet;

The symptoms of type 2 diabetes can be controlled over time with the Keto diet

Energy: Fats are more effective and long lasting source molecules to be burned as fuel by our bodies. Since they are a more dependable source of energy, you should feel even more energized on the Ketogenic Diet.

Hunger: Fats keep us satiated for longer hours and we feel hungry less often. Obviously, when we consume less, we gain less weight.

Acne: On a keto diet, you can recognize a drop in skin inflammation and acne lesions in just 12 weeks.

Why physical performance goes down temporarily on a ketogenic diet:

When you begin any new diet, your body needs time to adapt to it. This is also the case with the Ketogenic Diet. When you first start eating food high in fats and low in carbohydrates, you may see some limitations to the physical performance of your body. However, as soon as your body completely adapts to using fats as the main source of energy, you will start to regain your endurance and strength very quickly.

Many people are curious about whether they need carbohydrates to build strength and muscles. Absolutely not. When you work out to make muscles, you need to understand how your body processes food to gain mass and strengthen up well. Protein is the key.

Your body storage of glycogen can be refilled when you are on the Ketogenic Diet. This diet allows you to build good muscles, but there is a trick. You have to keep a check on your protein intake. Experts suggest that you must take in between 1.0-1.2 grams of protein for each lean pound of your body mass. You might find it difficult to gain mass on the Ketogenic Diet because the total fat in your body does not increase on the Ketogenic Diet. If for any reason you want to put on weight, you can do it through the Targeted Keto Diet or the Cyclical Keto Diet.

You might encounter some people who argue that performance is affected while you are on a Ketogenic diet. This is not entirely true. There was a study performed on trained cyclists undergoing the Ketogenic Diet. The results showed that their aerobic endurance remained good and was not affected at all. Also, their muscle mass remained the same as it had been when they had started. The cyclists' bodies adapted to the diet through ketosis, and their bodies limited glycogen and glucose storage and utilized fats for converting into energy.

During the time of the research, this group of cyclists was fed on a rigorous diet of proteins, green vegetables, and a good quantity of fats. Thus, even when you do more cardio exercises, the Ketogenic Diet helps you a lot.

The only time when ketosis can make you suffer in performance is when you need give explosive performance. When you need some boost in your workouts, you may take in more carbohydrates by consuming 25-30 grams of the same approximately 30 minutes prior to your training.

Hazards of a ketogenic diet:

You will probably find many people trying to scare you away from a low carbohydrate diet. But don't worry; they're likely under some misconceptions which are more famous than the Keto Diet itself. There have been hundreds of studies conducted with people who have followed the Keto Diet. The studies and research have proved that fewer carbohydrates and more fats are beneficial for health.

Strangely, people confuse the Ketogenic diet with a high carbs and high fats diet- a combination which is dreadful for the body. Obviously, when you eat tremendous amounts of food rich in fats as well as sugars, you are heading towards trouble.

If you have been thinking about going on a low fat diet, please think again. The Ketogenic Diet has been proven to be more effective for losing weight than a low fat diet. If you consume foods rich in carbohydrate content, your body produces glucose naturally. As we have already mentioned, our body finds it easiest to process carbohydrates and therefore, the body will look for them first. This results in immediate storage of excess fat in different parts of the body. This makes you gain weight and also gifts you with other ailments correlated with a high carbs-high fat diet, but not with the Ketogenic Diet.

Just to be safe, please check with a physician if you have any doubts about starting the Ketogenic Diet. You will also need to take precautions if you have a family history of diabetes or kidney ailments, because if you take in more proteins, it will put more strain on the kidneys.

High blood sugar, heart disease and high cholesterol are not the things you need to be concerned about. A high fat, low carbs diet is documented and known for improving blood sugar, cholesterol and reducing heart risks in your body.

What changes does your body undergo during the Ketogenic Diet?

Our bodies are adapted to the simplest routine of processing carbohydrates and utilizing them as energy. As a result, the body has an army of enzymes which are used in this metabolism, while it has only a small amount of enzymes which process fats. Even the enzymes which process the fats, mostly have the job of storing them.

When our bodies suddenly have to adapt to a shortage of glucose and high levels of fats, it is a lot of work for our bodies. They have to build a new army of enzymes adaptive to process fats. However, God has gifted us with amazing bodies which can do wonders when called on to adapt to any situation.

When our bodies are pushed into a state of ketosis, they naturally use what is remaining of the glucose. This implies that our bodies will exhaust up all the glycogen from our muscles, which can temporarily cause weakness or a feeling of low energy. You might feel lethargic for a few days. In the initial few weeks, you may experience mental fogginess, headaches, symptoms of flu (also called Keto-flu), irritability, and dizziness. Some people also called it a PMS for all!

Usually, these sicknesses are a result of your body flushing out electrolytes. Therefore, you may also pass more urine in the initial days of the Ketogenic Diet. You must ensure that you keep up your intake of sodium, and drink plenty of water. You can increase your salt consumption to large amounts. Take salt with everything possible. Doesn't that sound good? You do not have to keep any check on your salt intake. Salt helps your body to retain water and also helps to replenish electrolytes.

The average person who begins the Ketogenic Diet will take approximately 2 weeks to cut down his carbohydrate intake to 25-40 grams. However, it is best if you can cut down the carb intake to as low as 15 grams so that you can get on the right track in just one week. Therefore, the less time you take to reach the state of ketosis, the less time you will have to bear the feeling of sickness.

If you are a regular gym goer, you may notice that you may lose a little endurance and strength at first. As already mentioned, this is normal for everyone. However, you will soon reach sustainable levels of energy throughout the day.

Chapter 4

What, apart from willpower, is needed to start the Ketogenic Diet?

How to get started

When you eat fat rich foods, consume moderate amounts of proteins and few carbs, it has a massive effect on your health. You are already aware of the benefits of the Ketogenic Diet, despite its initial side effects. In the initial weeks, you might crave carbohydrates, but that phase will pass gradually. Artificial sweeteners are linked with sugar cravings. Thus, if you usually consume diet sodas or artificial sweeteners, you will need to flush them out of your system. Having a strong willpower and the right diet chart will help you transform your eating philosophies.

Did you cheat on your diet chart?

Hmm… So, you have finally cheated on your Keto Diet. It's okay once in a while. But ideally, this should not go on forever. If you have been off the track for a few days, you will definitely want to get back to your healthy Keto regime as soon as possible. Obviously, it feels good when you know that you are healthy from the inside.

It sounds simple, but sometimes it can be a monumental challenge. Once you cheat just for a non-Keto meal, you feel dreadful the next morning. You might feel bloated, shaky, and exhausted. Yes, it happens. Remember, when you switched to the Keto Diet, you felt the same sickness. Now when your body has adapted to the Ketogenic Diet, it will definitely shake when it does not get its regular diet of fats.

So, now you know that since you have cheated once, you might do it again. Thus, it is better to be prepared for the next time. Take a look at the following tips and note down whichever you find appropriate for you.

Whatever you like to do, do not beat yourself up

This is the most important advice given to ketogenic followers. There is a large group of ketogenic disciples who blame themselves for not having enough willpower to manage their new diet. Well, you are a human being and all of us fail sometimes. There is nothing to blame yourself about. We live in a world full of gluten and sugar. We have to face the temptation daily at some place or the other. If you do not give in to these temptations even 80% of times, you are a winner. It is an achievement to have even this much willpower.

Suppose your friend cheated once on their diet. Would you beat them? Never... So why do you do it to yourself? Just keep on trying!

Be responsible for your behavior

Do not take the first tip as an excuse. If you ate a bowlful of ice-cream at the party last night, take responsibility for it. If your body feels awful after cheating, positively take responsibility for it. Make a note of situations when you are tempted to cheat. For example, when you leave home for the office, do not forget to take some fat bombs along. If you are tempted to eat due to emotions, or due to boredom, or for some other reason, note down such situations and be prepared for them in advance. Don't allow yourself to become too hungry- when you are already full, you will be less likely to stuff yourself more.

Either have a salad for breakfast or do not have breakfast after a night of cheating

After you have cheated on the Keto Diet, you must take a strictly Keto meal after that. If you had a non-Keto meal at night, you might even like to skip your breakfast the next day. Intermittent fasting has been recognized as a healthy practice worldwide. You can eat later when you truly feel hungry. Do not eat just for the sake of eating. Eat when your body demands it. You will not feel weak at all.

Also, eating a plate full of Keto vegetables is just like healing your stomach after you have had an unhealthy meal. But, eat it only if you feel like eating. You will feel rejuvenated.

Make notes

Remember the good old school days when you used to make notes for every important thing so that you could cram them for exams? Similarly, you just need to note down the good as well as bad feelings you have towards your ketogenic regime. Fix a day in the week to write down your feelings briefly.

If you felt good for several weeks, write it down. If you felt awful after a meal of cheating, then write it down immediately. It is easy to forget your bad feelings once you overcome the inflammation, headaches and stomachaches. This simple practice of writing will give you a much more real and objective picture of your diet.

Go get moving

When you run or take a brisk walk for a few kilometers to get rid of the hangover after too much to drink, it helps your body break down all the harmful material you dumped into it the previous night. The same process works for food hangovers too. When you have a heavy, unhealthy meal, make sure that you make some time to work out. It does not have to be a vigorous workout, but should at least raise your heart rate a little and work out your bowels. You will definitely feel better once you make this a habit.

Cut down on alcohol

There is no doubt that alcohol is a toxic substance, even if it is just wine. When you take in alcohol, especially hard drinks, you have a high chance of losing your willpower and cheating on your meals. Thus, it is better to have as little alcohol as you can. Moreover, if you do take it, make sure that you digest it properly and get rid of the hangover.

Sip low carb liquids and lots of water frequently

It is advice given regularly by all dieticians, but it needs to be repeated often. We cannot emphasize this fact enough that you can flush out all the unhealthy molecules in your body by drinking appropriate amounts of water. If you are prone to boredom eating and feel like you want to stuff your mouth with something every hour, then you should rather choose warm water or flavored cold water over snacks. Look for your favorite flavors of herbal tea without sweeteners.

If you need something more satisfying, you can try sipping some warm bone broth. This will fill you up without adding any extra carbs to your diet. You can also add some turmeric to the bone broth to add flavor and take advantage of its anti-inflammatory properties.

Do not leave home hungry

When you leave home, make sure that you eat something healthy first. When you leave on an empty stomach, you will be more tempted to grab a burger or other fast food. You succumb to your temptations more easily when you are hungry. When you do not feel hungry, you have 90% less chance of cheating on Keto.

Do not punish or deprive yourself

Do not go overboard with the Ketogenic Diet and become a maniac. Just because you have started a healthy diet does not mean that you cannot eat when you want to. As already mentioned, if you are prone to boredom eating or emotional eating, keep some healthy substitutes with you. If you feel hungry, then please eat. Eating only a plate of salad a day for weeks at a time is not a good idea at all. These kinds of habits eventually make you even more prone to giving in to your temptations.

Find a support group or a buddy

There are many benefits to doing the Keto Diet with friends or with a support group. You get the required emotional support and you become accountable to someone. It is sometimes really difficult to keep promises to yourself. When you make a promise to your conscience, it is much easier to pretend that you never made it and you can just break it anytime. When you declare it to someone else, you feel more strongly that you have to abide by it.

If you cannot find any real friends to support you, you can join any online forum. Such virtual support is also helpful, because obviously real people are there on the other end. You can also get some amazingly easy recipes from these forums.

Develop cooking as a hobby

If you have been shying away from cooking throughout your life, now is the right time to pick the hobby up. When you cook something amazing, you feel encouraged to try and cook even more. Motivate yourself and look for some easy and fun recipes to support your Ketogenic Diet.

Chapter 5

What are the common mistakes committed by Keto followers?

As we have already mentioned before, if you have any doubts about the Ketogenic Diet, you must consult your physician. This high fat and low carb diet does not suit everyone. Though you probably know all the benefits of the Ketogenic diet, you also need to know where you can go wrong. Ketones are really beneficial as a fuel for the diaphragm and the heart. The state of ketosis can provide you with great cognitive performance and a good amount of focus. If you are an endurance athlete, this diet can prove extremely beneficial for distance swimming, cycling, ultra-running, or marathons.

However, there are not many resources available around us that can lead us to ketosis without experiencing nutrition deficiency if your Ketogenic diet goes wrong. Moreover, these deficiencies can get really big if you work out a lot. In addition, consuming MCT oil and coconut oil can get really, really boring very soon.

So, you must be thinking, "If there are so many stumbling blocks in my way to reaching the state of ketosis, is this diet worth the effort?" Yes, it is, definitely. It is not as difficult as it sounds. But it is crucial to have a basic understanding of the metabolism of your body and its nutritional needs before your march ahead with this diet plan.

You must also find out about the common mistakes committed by people who are already following this diet. Prepare yourself with a lot of ketogenic recipes and then go ahead and begin your new lifestyle.

Mistake No.1   Being afraid of fat

Obviously you know that you need to consume more fats than ever in the Ketogenic Diet. But the fact is that most of us are not able to overcome the mental block of thinking of fats as evil. The food industry has brainwashed us for many decades that we need to consume as few fats as we can in order to remain healthy. But the fact is that even on a non-Keto diet, we must consume some amount of fats to remain healthy. Even more in the Ketogenic Diet, where we have to derive our energy from fatty acids instead of glucose, we have to consume even more fats without any guilt. Since we are not consuming many carbohydrates, we must not shy away from fats.

Eat full fat cheese, eat the skin of the chicken, soak the broccoli in butter…. yeah… you are right. You have to eat as much fat as you can. The only fats you need to keep away from are vegetable oils like corn and canola. Such oils do not help cure inflammation in our bodies.

Even when you see that you need to consume massive amounts of meat and oils, try to remember that fat is not "evil" for your body. But do consume fats under the right guidance. You would not like to end up getting sick.

Mistake No.2   Consuming an excess of protein

Beginners of the Ketogenic Diet make another common blunder of replacing carbohydrates with proteins. This can lead you to gluconeogenesis, which means that amino acids are converted to glucose. But this is the exact opposite of what we need on a Ketogenic diet. We need to keep the glucose levels at a lower level and speed up the process of making ketones from fatty acids.

The fact is that you actually need to consume very small amounts of protein because fats are protein sparing. That means that our bodies' requirement of protein goes down with the high intake of fats. Thus, you do not need to worry if you are consuming fewer carbs. Do not try to compensate for them with proteins.

Mistake No. 3   Quitting too early

When you enter into the state of ketosis quickly, you might initially suffer from side effects. The changes in metabolism can be really dramatic because every cell of your body has to switch from the metabolism of glucose to fats. Your insulin levels go down due to lower levels of carbohydrates. This also affects your kidneys, which adapt to hold on to the sodium available in the body. When the insulin level is consistently low, the kidneys also shed sodium and water.

This is why it is always recommended that you consume more sodium and drink plenty of water, particularly in the initial phase. It helps to escape the Keto-flu. It is more appropriate if we call the symptoms "symptoms of carbohydrate withdrawal" due to the effect on electrolyte and hormonal balance.

These facts might seem intimidating to you. But you must pledge to yourself that you will not quit regardless of a little sickness in the initial days. You can consume strong bone broth containing high quality salt. You must also take a lot of rest and not work out intensely. Also, drink lots of water rich in minerals.

Moreover, the best advice is that you must go slowly when you begin the Ketogenic Diet. Do not give up when you feel sick during the first couple of weeks, and make sure you get all the recommended blood tests done. This will ensure that your body is not suppressing any health issues that do not appear on the surface.

Mistake No.4   Carbohydrates creep in

It sounds very obvious. But, it is not very simple as it sounds. Carbohydrates can seep in even from those sources which you think are carb-free. If you are fond of buying herbs, spices and vegetables, you might experience an increase in your carbs intake. Some products that you buy from the market with all the best intentions may contain carbs. For instance, factory made salad dressing, tomato sauces, substitutes for milk like almond milk and coconut milk have sugar added in them, meats such as duck meat, starchy vegetables, some kinds of herbal tea- these are just a few products which might contain carbohydrates.

It might become a challenge for you to eat out because many bars and restaurants use dressings, dips and sauces, which have additional sugar or honey. It definitely tastes good but is not good for your diet at all.

You must have solid, dependable information for restricting your carbohydrates intake, particularly in the initial phase when your body undergoes drastic changes.

Mistake No.5   Munching processed foods

This mistake is commonly committed by people who have read the Atkins diet (a low carb diet), and observed the foods which are sold online. No doubt that these foods keep your body at low carbohydrate levels and make your life a lot simpler. But the equally true fact is that these foods have high contents of artificial flavors, coloring, sucralose, polydextrose, and many other artificial sweeteners. These things obviously play havoc with your mental and physical health.

You might feel that you are not familiar with half of the ingredients mentioned in the Keto diet list or you are not aware of the shops which supply them. Do yourself a favor and make an effort find them out. The rule of thumb of the Ketogenic Diet is that if you are not able to cook or bake a meal out of these ingredients, then you must keep away from them.

The time is not far away when most of the food companies will start manufacturing foods made out of real ingredients because the trend of being concerned about one's health is reaching its peak really fast. So, be patient and be the pioneer of the Ketogenic Diet among your friends. They should also feel motivated when they see your dedication.

Mistake No.6   Eating the same recipes time and again and panicking when faced with new recipes

In the initial phase, when you feel overwhelmed by eating low carbs foods, you might always want to eat the same "safe" line of foods habitually. This is because you do not have much knowledge and experience of ketogenic recipes. That is why it is always recommended that you prepare yourself with a lot of ketogenic recipes before you start.

Suppose you had to eat eggs and bacon for every breakfast and nuts for snacks all the time. Wouldn't you get bored in just a couple of days? This is really common with most Keto practitioners. Even if you are not a Keto follower, you cannot eat the same pizza for breakfast, lunch and dinner over and over again!

Even when you eat low carb foods in your new regime, you must focus on improving your health. This is possible only with a varied and nutritious diet. Every individual is different. If your Keto friend loves bacon for breakfast, you might not like it.

Eat what you love and keep changing your routine. The same routine causes boredom to set in. That's not the only problem, though. Eating the same foods over and over may also cause nutritional deficiencies in your body and you may even become intolerant towards some foods. This would happen especially if you are very stressed or if you are on any kind of medication.

Intolerance for food sets off cramps, bloating, constipation, diarrhea, and many other symptoms. This not only impacts the gut health but also your immune system. The best thing is to keep trying new Keto-friendly foods, even if you have not ever heard of them. For example, chicken liver is a relatively unfamiliar thing for most people. But it's easy to find and to prepare. The long list of Keto-friendly foods can be transformed into many delicious recipes. So don't just stick to a couple of recipes you know. That will make you quit even faster.

Mistake No.7   A lack of planning

One of the major stumbling blocks on the Ketogenic Diet is a lack of planning. If you do not plan well, there is a good chance that you will fail. For example, you are already aware that your kitchen should be well stocked with most of the Keto-friendly ingredients. But what happens when one day you realize that you do not have enough coconut milk in your fridge? You might panic and get frustrated because the shop near the corner street does not sell coconut milk.

Many Keto ingredients which are staples for a low carb diet such as oily fish, olives, coconut oil, ghee, etc. are available only online or in health shops. More supermarkets are coming up with ketogenic products nowadays. Still, you need to plan properly and be well aware that you would need these products. Thus, when you visit the shop next time that stocks Keto goods, you must buy more than you need for just a meal. You can also cook ketogenic recipes in bulk and save on your time as well as money.

Mistake No.8   Getting too obsessed with the diet

Another major obstacle in the Ketogenic diet is being too obsessed with the diet. You might love to plan every last bite of the day in the initial stages. However, this is not practicable. It is feasible though for those patients who have been recommended the Ketogenic Diet due to any medication or sickness like epilepsy. In such ailments, every bite has to be planned without any chance of failure. Otherwise the patient might have to face serious consequences.

However, since you have chosen the Ketogenic Diet yourself, you must not get too stressed over your dietary changes. The new routine should not interfere with your mental balance. Do not become a maniac thinking what your next meal should be or how you can increase your ketones or what you should eat on the vacation next weekend!

In order to avoid such craziness, you should sometimes just relax and make a few recipes without counting and weighing. You can also give yourself some more time if you feel so and do not feel guilty about it. If you remain under mental stress about your food, you will not be able to enjoy the physical benefits of the Ketogenic

Diet. Physical benefits take even more time to show up when you have mental turmoil going on.

Mistake No.9   Ignoring the warning signs of your body

People who get obsessed with the changes in their diets can end up measuring ketones and blood glucose in their body and weighing the food every time, making exact plans for meals, etc. They are even literally scared of eating at restaurants where they cannot actually control their food. According to the experts, these people are the ones who mostly ignore the warning signs given by their body.

For example, perhaps you know that there is a particular ketogenic recipe that you do not like and your tummy feels bloated when you eat it. Still, you eat it because you "know" that it is good for your body. As a matter of fact, your body knows better than you do. Do not ignore the signs given by your body. If a food does not make you feel good from inside, then do not eat it.

In another instance, at some stage you might not feel like exerting your body to do high intensity training. If you go ahead just because it was on the chart for the day, you might end up hurting your ligaments.

No meal or training or expert advice can take over your innate intuition and knowledge. Do take the warning signs seriously and do not foolishly stick to your regime even when your body is telling you not to do so.

The Ketogenic Diet or other low carb diets are not suitable for everyone. If you do not feel better than before you switched to the Ketogenic Diet (after the initial phase of sickness, of course) you might like to reconsider your decision.

Mistake No.10   Giving in to social pressure

Our social lives are a big factor which should never underestimate. Even if our friends and family do not mean to pull us back from our healthy regime; they probably will not stop teasing us. We have to listen to comments like, "Oh, come on dear, you are here to party! Don't be a spoil sport. You will not die if you eat just one slice of pizza!" And so we give in.

It is of course impossible to try and explain about the Ketogenic Diet and its benefits every time. Nobody wants to listen to your blabbing and of course, you would also not like to show off your new lifestyle all the time. Although your family knows about the benefits you have experienced from the Ketogenic Diet, they probably still won't stop pushing you to have another piece of cake.

Furthermore, many medical professionals do not understand the true concept of the Ketogenic Diet. However, it is a well-established fact that you can go by the 80/20 rule, and this allows you to have some breaks and enjoy a few treats in moderate amounts. But, when you are completely in ketosis, you will probably find that you truly do not feel like eating anything apart from the stipulated foods. They actually do not make you feel good when you are in ketosis. When you eat a slice of cake during this state, it actually does not feel good.

Mistake No.11   Poor timing

Another crucial factor in determining the success of the Ketogenic Diet is the timing when you start it. You must consider the circumstances that are present when you are about to start this diet. Since the Ketogenic Diet demands a lot of attention, care and rest; you must not start at least a week before something important is expected. For example, if you have a very important meeting in your office next week, do not start it now.

Also, if you are going through a busy season professionally, you must not start this diet. You can begin this regime when you have ample time in hand to rest if you feel frail in the initial phase of keto. When off season times are going on in your profession, then you can think about starting it. This would allow you to take rest or even a holiday if you cannot work at all.

Mistake No.12   Not providing enough time for the body to transition

In the initial week, your bowel habits may change. You may experience constipation or diarrhea, but it will regulate over time. For some people, fiber supplements help in curing stomach problems. But, for others, fiber may not help at all. Thus, you may want to seek personal advice from your physician before eating lots of fiber.

The adaptation may even take up to a month. Many people also experience an energy blast, euphoric feelings, along with a lot of fat loss. Your urine may smell strange and you might also develop some kind of metallic taste in the mouth. However, you do not have to be worried. These changes are a sign that your new diet is working.

Mistake No. 13   Testing ketosis with urine ketone testing sticks

This is a big mistake some people make. Low carbohydrate diet followers have relied on the urine ketone testing sticks for a very long time. These sticks test the level of acetoacetate your boy is excreting. You may find it extremely thrilling to see the sticks turn dark purple from light pink. It makes you feel good about your body, but unfortunately, these sticks do not show exact results. Moreover, they cannot show the particular type of ketones your body uses as a fuel.

A more accurate test is the blood test for checking beta-hydroxybutyrate. It will give you a better picture of whether you are adapted to keto or not, or if your body is burning ketones and fat for fuel- which is the actual essence of the Ketogenic Diet.

The information you gain about blood ketones rather than urine ketones is absolute gold regarding your performance on your low carbohydrate diet.

Mistake No. 14   Eating too much or too often

It is very common in our society to eat by the clock and to eat much more than it is required to feed our stomachs. You have probably been doing this on your high-carb diet. But it is a blunder if you do the same with your ketogenic diet. When you eat a high fat and low carb diet, your body really does not require food for many hours in a row. So do not feel worried about it. People often indulge in three full meals in a day along with snacks. Trust the experts' advice, they would never recommend that you eat this much every day.

Your body can eat up the fats it has stored for energy and sustain effectively. You would not feel deprived even if you do not eat. You have to eat food only when you feel hungry.

Mistake No. 15   Falling short of maintaining blood sugar levels

You must be thinking, "Why do I have to measure my blood sugar when I am not a diabetic?" The fact is that every one of us should keep a check on it. When your blood sugar is normalized during ketosis, it keeps your hunger down, regulates your mood and gives you a sense of well-being. Moreover, when your blood sugar is regulated, it is easier to attain nutritional ketosis and vice versa.

Chapter 6

How can you avoid Ketogenic Diet mistakes?

By now, you must have got an idea that you need tons of patience and perseverance to stay healthy with the Ketogenic Diet. Besides this, you also need a few tricks and tips mentioned in the previous chapters to stick to this new lifestyle. It is easy to give in to social pressure and your own temptations, but you have to be determined and convince your friends and family that this is not just a new fad and that you truly want to transform your body for good.

This can happen only when you are yourself convinced that you have chosen the right track. When your family members see the changes in your body and your health, they might also get motivated to adapt this way of eating.

You have already read the common mistakes people commit. To avoid these pitfalls, you must keep the points listed below in mind. Even if you find them repetitive, they have been mentioned to stress the facts you need to remember at all times.

Give yourself enough time to adapt

Never ever start the Ketogenic Diet if you do not have enough time to give to your body for adaptation. You must have at least a couple of weeks in hand to overcome the keto fever and other symptoms like constipation and diarrhea. It's probably best not to start this routine just a week before your holiday. It might spoil your holiday mood and make you feel low.

Such things discourage you a lot and get you off the track sooner than ever. You must be motivated enough to keep up with anything new that you pick up.

Ask for support from your friends and family

Since you may also experience mood swings due to the drastic changes in your diet, you may want to inform some of your loved ones about your new routine and ask for their cooperation and support.

Your true well-wishers will be more than happy to help you in this important step of your life. You can also ask them to prohibit you from indulging in non-keto food even when you feel tempted to do so.

They may tease you at times, but do not feel disheartened. Be brave and take it in good spirits. When you give cheerful replies to people, they are even happier with you. When you are in a bad mood, alert them of the situation and tell them to beware of you! You would not like to spoil your relationships forever just because of a couple of hours of mood swings. When you take proper precautionary steps without worrying too much, you are bound to succeed.

Stay around motivating factors

You must make friends with people who are positive in their lives and do not pull you down all the time. If you stay around negative people, they might turn out to not be your well-wishers. They are not happy to see anyone succeed and will be happy if you fail.

On the other hand, positive people themselves want to succeed in the smallest things in their lives and are happy to see others do so. They encourage you to keep trying even after you fall at times. They will encourage you to rise up and double your efforts. Spend time with both types of people for one week in your life before starting this routine and you will definitely see the difference the two groups make to your outlook.

Keep visiting the physician

Do not ignore this piece of advice. You might think that you have read enough and gained much knowledge from people around you, but it is always advisable to seek the advice of a physician you trust. It is worth spending the money in advance rather than thinking of saving it. If you end up making any major mistakes in the Ketogenic Diet, you may have to face some serious consequences and pay much more money than you should have.

Also, it is important to visit a trustworthy physician. He must be able to diagnose you properly and give required advice. There are some physicians who deliberately give you the wrong advice so that you fail frequently and visit them more often so that they can make more money. Beware of such doctors.

If you do not have a family physician in your vicinity, ask your friends who have been following the Ketogenic Diet lately. By all means, get help from internet forums, but please also follow the advice of your doctor.

Do not go maniac

Yes, you have taken a major step in your life, but nobody would like to see you going nuts over this new ketogenic diet. This fact cannot be stressed enough that we advocate this diet only to see you healthier, and not to see you getting obsessed with ketones and ketosis. You need to make peace with your eating habits. If you do not feel motivated enough to follow this regime, think again if you really want to do it for the rest of your life.

Your body must feel good after making so much effort. If this is not the case, you must seek the advice of your friends and family who have the know-how of the Ketogenic Diet. They might enlighten you if you are not able to decide. But do give yourself ample time to adjust before you want to re-think.

It is always easy to step back once you have decided to do something, but it is not so easy to get back to the same milestone once you have crossed it.

Keep yourself well equipped

As you must have already read, keep your kitchen well stocked in advance so that you do not fall short of supplies when you need to cook anything. Since this diet is almost entirely based on fats, it might prove a little expensive for you. Thus, it is better to buy things in larger quantities to save money. Groceries always prove cheaper when bought in bigger packets and of course, they last much longer.

Find stores online which keep groceries specifically for the Ketogenic Diet. You'll probably get your stuff from such stores at much cheaper rates than you would at the local supermarket. Such stores cater to the needs of the Ketogenic Diet followers and stock products required by them. They also procure the groceries at cheaper prices and hence supply them to you at comparatively competitive rates. An occasional supplier of ketogenic supplies will charge much higher than the things are worth. Hence, make an effort and find out places that suit you and your budget.

When you keep the pitfalls and precautionary measures in mind, you will be less likely to fail. It is always better to be well prepared rather than repent later. Keep on the right track and you will definitely reap the fruits soon.

Conclusion

After reading this entire book on the Ketogenic Diet: Ketogenic Diet Mistakes You Need to Know, you must be feeling more at ease. It is always good to hear from a reliable source about an important thing that you have been anxious about. The Ketogenic Diet is not at all mysterious in itself but people who have not succeeded in it, have made it so. They have spread such myths about the Ketogenic Diet that even those who have the guts to start it, have to think twice before doing it.

All of us have at least enough willpower to take any new step. The rest of the journey is covered with the help of new milestones and support from our family and friends. You do not need to panic about this diet. Every single human being among us is capable of achieving much more they can imagine. Even the biggest deeds of the world were started as baby steps towards achieving something new. Perseverance and good intentions lead people to achieve what they have always wanted.

Have you ever read the autobiography of an athlete or an Olympic winner? Most of them come from humble backgrounds. They just have big dreams. In the initial stages of their career, even they are doubtful about their success, but as the time passes and they stay patient and keep up the hard work, all their efforts pay off well.

Similarly, even if you are an ordinary person with no Olympic aspirations, you cannot underestimate your determination and your motivation. All of us want to have a healthy body and remain disease free throughout our lives. But only a few of us are able to achieve it. It's not that those who have been successful in achieving the state of ketosis have not faced any obstacles. It is just a matter of facing these troubles bravely and overcoming your temptations. The victorious keto-followers have resisted their temptations well. Eventually, when you are able to say, "No, thank you" to mouthwatering cuisines for quite some time, you even start disliking that type of food.

Thus, just keep your eyes on the end results that you are going to have a good body once you have your ketones working for you instead of carbohydrates. I'm sure you will be able to make an effort with even more dedication than you think. Good luck with this life transforming ketogenic diet!

Book 3:

Ketogenic Diet for Beginners

That You Can Prep In 15 Minutes Or Less

By Emily Simmons

Introduction

A completely new lifestyle is waiting for you! This book is written strictly according to the ketogenic diet. You will find an entire range of ketogenic recipes. If you are new to the ketogenic concept, the basic thing is that this diet plan is based on a high fat and low carbohydrate intake. Thus, do not get intimidated by the cheese and meat recipes in this book if you are presently on a low-fat weight loss regime. Don't worry. We won't tell you anything which makes you gain weight.

We have not kept any secrets about the ketogenic diet. Since it is an entirely new diet, your body will need time to adapt. You'll have to be patient for about 2-3 weeks until it becomes a habit to eat negligible amounts of carbohydrates. But ultimately, you will start feeling good about your body. The energy you get from these foods is mobilized from the fats you receive. You will feel energetic as well as satiated for hours at your workplace or home. Thus, you will not get those cravings for eating so frequently that you get when you are on a high carbohydrate diet.

Carbohydrates do provide energy to your body, but they do not keep you full for long. The fats that are received along with carbohydrates are stored around your stomach and thighs until needed. However, with the ketogenic diet, you do not have to worry while indulging in fatty foods. We will explain to you how the diet works in more detail in section 1 of this book. Therefore, you will not be blindly following the high fat and low carbohydrate diet, but will have a good understanding of how it works.

What is the Ketogenic Diet?

The ketogenic diet is high in fats and moderate in proteins but low in carbohydrates. The diet is typically designed so that the body burns the fat in the food and not the carbohydrates. Hence, the carbohydrate is converted into forms of glucose. The glucose gets transported throughout the body and plays a very important role in the functioning of the brain. This metabolism is called ketosis.

Ketosis is a process that naturally benefits the body. The human body adapts itself to ketosis when food is not available. The same process is utilized in the modern world to lose weight naturally. Ketone bodies show improvement in diseases and thus we naturally stay immune. The diet is used to treat even extreme medical conditions like epilepsy, diabetes, Alzheimer's, autism, cancer, etc.

However, it is highly advised that you do not blindly follow the ketogenic diet plan. There are many different ketogenic diet charts, but you can choose the one which is most suitable for you. The most famous ketogenic diet is the Atkins diet. The main concern of the ketogenic diet is the amount of carbohydrates to be consumed per day. The diet plan is based on the monitoring of the intake of carbohydrates in a day, which is ideally just 20-60 grams. The protein intake is moderate and depends upon how much exercise you do and what your gender and height are. The balance of calories is obtained from fats. Once you start the ketogenic diet, your objective should be to follow it for as long as possible.

The intake of nutrients in a ketogenic plan is as follows: 70-75% of the calories are obtained from fats, 20-25% from proteins and 5-10% from carbohydrates. The calories are unrestricted in such a diet. Your hunger reduces in this diet plan. Thus, it's up to you whether you count your calories or not.

Things to remember before following the ketogenic diet and why should you consume high fat with moderate levels of proteins?

Fats do not affect blood insulin and sugar levels. Proteins do affect insulin as well as blood sugar if consumed in large quantities. High levels of insulin can restrict the ability of the body to burn and release fatty acids that provide necessary elements required for ketosis. Some people might be affected by it more than others depending upon how much they exercise. Moreover, following a diet with high levels of lean protein and not enough fats might make you ill with a strange health condition called "rabbit starvation". The concept to remember therefore for those who want to lose fat while maintaining blood sugar levels is that you should eat fat to lose more fat.

Targeted Ketogenic Diet and Cyclical Ketogenic Diet

There are two types of diets for people who exercise regularly. The targeted ketogenic diet is one where you consume carbohydrates just before and just after your regime of workouts. This plan suits those who are involved in doing intense workouts daily and require some carbohydrate as fuel.

The cyclical ketogenic diet is one where you consume a minimum amount of carbohydrates per day. On weekends, you consume relatively higher quantities of carbohydrates in order to refill your store of muscle glycogen. This is done to maintain the energy levels in your body for the workouts you do.

Who should follow the ketogenic diet?

Doctors typically recommend this diet for those children whose seizures do not respond to various seizure medicines. Children suffering with Lennox-Gastaut syndrome are particularly prescribed with this medicine.

Usually, adults have not in the past followed these diets. Still, there are many examples, where adults have also benefitted from this. Since there are many live examples around us, the trend of the ketogenic diet is catching on.

Epilepsy conditions in particular may be improved with the ketogenic diet. In brief, anyone can follow this diet unless there are some particular reasons not to follow it.

Benefits of the ketogenic diet

Low carbohydrate diets have been controversial since the time they emerged. However, the fact is that many human studies have proved that they are beneficial in many ways. Let's take a look at some of the benefits:

The ketogenic diet kills excessive appetite for all the right reasons. It makes you feel full for longer.

You can lose weight faster than those on active diet plans.

This diet is very effective in reducing the abdominal fat that is harmful for the body.

It reduces the risk of heart diseases.

Your levels of insulin and blood sugar are improved.

Those suffering with high blood pressure experience improvement.

Many brain disorders are proven to have been cured by ketogenic diets.

Dangers of the ketogenic diet

If you have kidney problems, the high protein levels of the ketogenic diet may worsen the problem.

Kidney stones are likely to get worse due to the excessive urinating of calcium.

If you do not consume fiber in your diet, too much meat may not prove good for your gut health; increased acid formation due to excessive consumption of meat and no fiber.

Again, low consumption of fruits and vegetables causes inflammation.

Side effects of the ketogenic diet

It is a little difficult to switch to the ketogenic diet plan. Therefore it will help to know about a few side effects that you might face in the first week of beginning a ketogenic diet. You can then be prepared for them beforehand and take some precautions to avoid them.

It becomes easy to cure the side effects if you know the reasons behind them. Your body needs some time to switch from your regular diet and adjust itself to burn fat and not glucose. It need some time to create some enzymes.

Frequent urination

You might use the bathroom more often than before a day after you start this diet. This is because your body burns glucose that is stored in your muscles and liver. This process releases more water.

Dizziness and fatigue

When your body dumps water, minerals like potassium, salt and magnesium are also lost. This may cause dizziness and fatigue. You can avoid these side effects by consuming more minerals found in various food sources. Drink salty broth or flavor your food with more salt. Consume foods with more potassium. Leafy vegetables are a major source of potassium.

Make a note to consult your doctor if you are under medication for high blood pressure, kidney ailments or heart diseases.

Low blood sugar

When you have a diet rich in carbohydrates, your body keeps some insulin aside to absorb the sugar which is created from the carbohydrate. But, during the ketogenic diet, you might experience low blood sugar because of lower carbohydrate levels. Eating frequently helps to cure this side effect.

Headache

Due to the loss of a few minerals, you might experience headaches in the initial days. Again, drinking salty broth helps in this condition. If nothing else helps, you may add a little carbohydrate to your diet.

Constipation

Apart from other things, constipation is the most common side effect that happens to the new followers of the ketogenic diet due to an imbalance of magnesium and potassium. You can cut down on your consumption of nuts and drink a lot of water to avoid constipation.

Sugar Cravings

The more you are deprived of something, the more your body craves it. Only time can heal this problem. Thus, we stress that you need to have strong willpower to control your cravings.

Coconut Oil Fried Veggies and Eggs

This recipe will never bore you. It keeps you full for a very long time so you won't crave a mini burger every two hours!

SERVES:	2
PREPARATION TIME:	15 min

INGREDIENTS:

Coconut oil	2 tablespoons
Spinach	1 cup
Frozen mixed vegetables	1-2 cups
Salt	½ teaspoon
Pepper	¼ teaspoon
Eggs	3-4

METHOD:

Thaw the frozen vegetables.

Preheat the frying pan and pour in the coconut oil.

Add thawed vegetables. Stir well.

Whisk eggs and add to the frying pan. Stir well.

Sprinkle salt and pepper on the vegetables.

Add chopped spinach to the mixture. Stir properly with the eggs. Stir fry the mixture until the eggs are ready.

Grilled Chicken Wings with Salsa and Veg

Chicken is always tasty, no matter what form you get it in. The salsa sauce and a mix of spices make this dish special.

SERVES: 2-3

PREPARATION TIME: 15 min for preparation, 1 hour for baking and refrigerating

INGREDIENTS:

Chicken wings	500 grams
Spice mix teaspoons	2-3

Cauliflower	½ cup
Bell peppers	½ cup
Beans	¼ cup
Cucumber	½ cup
Tomato	½ cup
Salsa	3 tablespoons
Salt	1.5 teaspoons
Pepper	1 teaspoon

METHOD:

Marinate the chicken wings by sprinkling the spice mix on them.

Preheat the oven to 180-200 degrees.

Once oven has heated, put the chicken into the oven for approximately 40 minutes.

You must grill the wings till they become crunchy and brown.

Take a skillet and stir-fry the chopped vegetables-cauliflower, bell pepper, beans, cucumber, and tomato. Cook them till crisp.

Sprinkle salt and pepper over the vegetables.

Take them off the heat and let them cool.

You can also refrigerate the vegetables if you like for an hour. Take the chicken out of the oven and serve hot with chilled vegetables and salsa.

Eggs and Bacon

Though bacon is a processed meat, it is low in carbohydrate content. Thus, you can consume it once or twice a week if you want to lose weight. Besides, it tastes good!

SERVES:	2
PREPARATION TIME:	15 min

INGREDIENTS:

Bacon	8 ounces
Eggs	3-4
Garlic powder	½ teaspoon
Onion powder	½ teaspoon
Spice mix	1 teaspoon

Sea salt teaspoon	½
Pepper	¼ teaspoon

METHOD:

Preheat a pan and pour in a teaspoon of coconut oil.

Put in bacon and stir-fry until it becomes tender.

Sprinkle spice mix, onion powder and garlic powder onto bacon and mix.

Take the bacon out on a plate when ready.

Scramble the eggs and stir-fry in the bacon fat. Add sea salt and pepper and mix well till cooked through.

Serve hot on plate with bacon.

Ground Beef & Bell Peppers

This is a delicious beef meal that you can eat whenever you want. Take any leftovers to work in your lunchbox the next day.

SERVES:	2
PREPARATION TIME:	15 min

INGREDIENTS:

Coconut oil teaspoons	2
Ground beef ounces	5-6
Sliced Onions	1-2 medium
Red chili teaspoon	½

Coriander teaspoon	¼
Bay leaves	2
Clove powder	¼ teaspoon
Cinnamon powder teaspoon	¼
Sliced bell peppers	1
Spinach	½ cup

METHOD:

Preheat a frying pan and pour coconut oil into it.

Put in the bay leaves and stir.

Put the sliced onions into the oil and sauté.

Add ground beef to the pan and stir.

Add the spices (red chili, coriander, clove powder and cinnamon powder) to the mixture and mix well.

Add spinach.

Cook until beef becomes tender. Place on a serving plate.

Put sliced bell peppers into the remaining oil in the frying pan and sauté for a minute or so.

Serve on top of the beef.

Low-Carb No Bun Cheeseburgers

This recipe is low on carbohydrate intake because there is no grain-bun used in the dish. The melted cheese on the top is a delicious treat. It is difficult to get bored with this amazing mouth-watering cheeseburger.

SERVES:	2
PREPARATION TIME:	15 min
INGREDIENTS:	

Butter	2 tablespoons
Frozen Hamburgers	2
Cheddar cheese tablespoon	1

Cream cheese	1 tablespoon
Salsa	2 tablespoon
Spice mix	1-2 teaspoons
Spinach	½ cup

METHOD:

Preheat a frying pan and put some butter in it.

Put two burgers in the butter and fry them for 2-3 minutes or until they are brown.

Flip them over and fry from on the other side too.

When they are light brown in color, put the spice mix on the burgers.

Add some cheddar cheese slices and some chunks of cream cheese. Do not stir.

Turn down the flame or heat and let the cheese melt.

Take the hamburgers out on a plate and serve them with shredded spinach.

Pour some of the fat left in the frying pan over the spinach as well as a dressing.

Top the burgers with salsa to make them even juicier.

Fried Chicken Breasts

Chicken breasts are so juicy and yummy that they can be had anytime of the day. You do not have to think twice before making this quick dish.

SERVES: 2

PREPARATION TIME: 15 min

INGREDIENTS:

Butter	2 tablespoons
Chicken breasts ounces	6-8

Salt	2 teaspoons
Pepper	1 teaspoon
Garlic powder	½ teaspoon
Curry powder	½ teaspoon
Vegetables (bell pepper and onions)	½ cup

METHOD:

Cut the chicken breasts into small pieces.

Preheat a pan and add butter to it.

Add the pieces of chicken to the frying pan.

Add spices to the chicken- garlic powder, salt, pepper and curry.

Stir fry the chicken until it turns brown. You will notice a crunchy texture in the meat after a while.

Place it on a plate.

Put the sliced bell peppers and onions in the pan and sauté for 30 seconds.

Take the vegetables out and serve them with the chicken.

The chicken is already juicy in texture. So there is no need to add any sauce. Still, if you feel that it is dry, you can serve some salsa sauce along with it.

Fake Meat Pizza

You might have been missing pizza after switching to the ketogenic diet. Here we have a healthy solution for you. This meat-za is prepared with absolutely healthy ingredients with all the familiar flavors of a pizza. Moreover, you can modify this versatile recipe with as many ingredients as you want. Just indulge into it without any guilt.

SERVES: 2

PREPARATION TIME: 15 min

BAKING TIME: 40 min

INGREDIENTS:

Ground beef	5 ounces
Salsa	2-3 tablespoons
Onions	2-3 medium
Garlic powder	2 teaspoons
Shredded cheese	½ cup
Bacon	10-15 pieces
Spice mix	2 teaspoons

METHOD:

Preheat the oven to 180-200 degrees.

Meanwhile, dice the onions and bacon.

Mix the onions, ground beef, salsa, garlic powder and spice mix in a bowl. Press onto the bottom of a greased round baking dish.

Put some shredded cheese on top of the mixture.

Spread the slices of bacon over the top.

Put the baking dish into the oven for 30-40 minutes or until the cheese and bacon look crunchy.

Take out the dish and serve wedges of this meat-za on a plate.

Cheesy Egg & Bacon

If you make this delicious egg and bacon just once, you'll make it over and over again. Don't worry, though- all the ingredients are good for you!

SERVES:	2
PREPARATION TIME:	15 min
INGREDIENTS:	
Eggs	6
Milk	1 cup
Melted butter	2 tablespoons

Chopped spring onions	¼ cup
Chopped bacon rashers	5
Grated cheese	1 cup
Chopped Cilantro	¼ cup

METHOD:

Preheat the oven to 180 degrees.

Take a frying pan and sauté bacon to render out the excess fat.

Take a medium sized bowl and whisk the eggs with butter and milk.

Season the mixture with pepper and salt.

Take a rectangular baking dish and pour the egg mixture into it.

Spread bacon rashers and cheese onto the dish. Sprinkle onions over evenly.

Put the baking dish in the oven and cook for 30-40 minutes. When the egg sets in the middle, remove from the oven.

Cut into portions and serve garnished with green cilantro.

May be served with a side of green salad.

Spicy Shrimp & Mashed Cauliflower

Shrimps are the perfect warm food for those cold autumn months. Moreover, in this recipe, you learn a substitute for starchy potatoes. We are giving you a recipe for cauliflower starch, which looks like mashed potato, tastes like mashed potato and satisfies your craving for starch like mashed potato does. When you are getting all the benefits of potatoes from cauliflower, then you can think about completely quitting potatoes.

SERVES: 2

PREPARATION TIME: 15 min

INGREDIENTS (for cauliflower mash):

Cauliflower florets	4 cups
Mayonnaise	1/3 cup

Peeled and minced garlic	1 clove
Water	1 tablespoon
Kosher salt	1 teaspoon
Black pepper	1/8 teaspoon
Lemon juice	¼ teaspoon
Lemon zest	½ teaspoon
Fresh chopped chives	1 tablespoon

INGREDIENTS (for shrimps):

Frozen shrimps	16 ounce
Butter	2 tablespoons
Salt	1 teaspoon
Pepper	½ teaspoon

| Sriracha chili sauce tablespoons | 2 |

METHOD (for cauliflower mash):

Take a large microwave-safe bowl and mix the mayonnaise, cauliflower, water, garlic, pepper and salt.

Microwave the mixture on high for nearly 12-15 minutes.

When the mixture becomes very soft, mash it with a potato masher if you like a coarse texture.

If you prefer a smooth texture, puree the mixture with a blender.

Add lemon juice, lemon zest and chives. Mix them well. Serve warm.

METHOD (for shrimps):

Take a large sauce pan and heat it over medium-high heat.

Put butter into it and let it melt.

Peel and thaw the shrimp. Toss into the pan and sauté.

Cook for about 4-6 minutes until the shrimps become pink.

Add salt and pepper to the shrimps and mix well.

Add the sriracha sauce and mix in. If you want a spicy dish, add more than 2 tablespoons of sauce.

Cook for another 2 minutes and then remove the pan from the heat.

Place some cauliflower mash in a plate and top it with shrimps. Enjoy!

Bacon & Brussels Sprouts

While Brussels sprouts aren't a complete dish on their own, you just need to add shallots, bacon and garlic to make a tasty main or side dish.

SERVES: 2

PREPARATION TIME: 15 min

INGREDIENTS:

Chopped bacon (center cut) slices — 6

Sliced shallots
 ½ cup

Brussels sprouts
 1.5 pounds

Thinly sliced garlic cloves
 6

Fat free chicken broth (lower sodium)
 ¾ cup

Salt
 1/8 teaspoon

Black pepper (freshly ground)
 1/8 teaspoon

METHOD:

Take a large skillet and heat it over medium heat.

Put bacon in, and cook for 5 minutes till brown.

Remove the pan from the heat.

Take out the bacon with a deep spoon.

Keep 1 tablespoon of dripping in the skillet and discard the rest.

Put the skillet back on the heat and put in bacon, Brussels sprouts and shallot. Sauté together for 4 minutes.

Add garlic and stir together for a few minutes.

Add chicken broth and let it boil.

Stirring now and then allow the broth to almost evaporate (takes about 2 minutes). The sprouts will become crisp-tender.

Sprinkle with pepper and salt and remove from heat.

Serve hot.

Easy & Quick Tomato Soup

Just look around your kitchen and refrigerator. You might find that you already have the ingredients for this quick and creamy soup recipe. This is a warming and healthy soup.

SERVES:	3
PREPARATION TIME:	15 min
INGREDIENTS:	
Butter	2 tablespoons
Onions	½ cup
Undrained diced tomatoes 28 ounces	1 can of
Chicken broth	2 cups

Heavy cream	1 cup
Salt	½ teaspoon
Pepper	¼ teaspoon
Minced parsley	2 tablespoons

METHOD:

Take a deep saucepan and heat it over a medium-high heat.

Put in the butter and let it melt.

Add onions and sauté them until they become tender.

Add tomatoes along with their liquid into the pan. Mix well and let the mixture boil.

Simmer on low heat for 5 minutes.

Turn off the heat and puree the mixture with a hand blender.

Add the cream and stir well.

Add seasoning and mix in.

Add parsley and serve hot.

Salami with Goat Cheese

Delicious rolls of rich salami combined with fresh arugula make a lovely dish for an afternoon meal. Not only they are carbohydrate free, they will keep you satiated for many hours. Moreover, the arugula in the rolls lowers high blood pressure and reduces the amount of oxygen a person needs during a work-out. It has also been proven to enhance performance during athletics.

SERVES: 5

PREPARATION TIME: 15 min

INGREDIENTS:

Genoa salami (thin slices)
    14 slices or 3.5 ounces

Goat cheese (fresh) ounces	3
Baby arugula	2 ounces
Olive oil (extra virgin) tablespoon	1
Vinegar (red wine) teaspoons	2
Kosher salt	½ teaspoon
Pepper teaspoon	¼

METHOD:

On a large tray, arrange the slices of salami in one layer.

Spoon a small heap of goats cheese in the middle of every slice.

Take a bowl and mix the arugula with vinegar and olive oil.

Season with pepper and salt.

Divide the arugula mixture onto all the salami slices. Roll the slices.

Cut the rolls in half. When you want to serve them, keep the seam down on the platter to prevent their opening, or tie up with chive leaves as illustrated.

Stuffed Deviled Eggs

These deviled eggs are ideal for kids' birthday parties. Not only they are quick to prepare, they are awesome to eat as well. If your kids find them too spicy, you can adjust the amounts of mayonnaise and mustard. You can also serve them to the adults garnished with finely chopped chives or parsley and paprika.

SERVES:	4
PREPARATION TIME:	15 min
COOKING TIME:	30 min
INGREDIENTS:	
Eggs	12
Mayonnaise tablespoons	2

Chinese mustard	1 teaspoon
Yellow mustard	2 teaspoons
Salt	as per taste
Pepper	as per taste
Paprika	½ teaspoon
Chopped chives	1 tablespoon

METHOD:

Take a large saucepan and place all the eggs in it.

Cover them with water and bring it to boil.

Remove the pan from the heat and cover it with a lid.

Let the eggs stand in the hot water for 10-12 minutes.

Remove the eggs from the water. Let them cool and then peel.

Slice the eggs lengthwise in half. Remove the yolks.

Put the yolks in a bowl and add mayonnaise.

Mash them with yellow mustard, Chinese mustard, pepper and salt.

Fill the egg whites which you hollowed earlier with this mixture of egg yolks. You can use a teaspoon or piping bag.

Sprinkle with paprika and chopped chives to garnish.

Refrigerate these eggs until you serve them.

Low Carb Chili Beef in Rich Tomato Gravy

This recipe takes a long cooking time but it is worth it. The preparation takes only 15 minutes. You will go back to this recipe again and again once you serve it to your family. The rich flavor of the tomato gravy is absolutely delicious.

SERVES: 4

PREPARATION TIME: 15 min

COOKING TIME: 2 hours
simmer cook

INGREDIENTS:

Ground beef pounds   1.25

Tomato paste   8 ounce

Chopped tomatoes   1.5

Chopped red bell pepper	1
Chopped onion	½ cup
Chopped celery sticks	2
Cumin seeds	1.5 teaspoons
Chili powder	1 teaspoon
Pepper	½ teaspoon
Salt	1 teaspoon
Water	¾ cup or more if needed

METHOD:

Preheat a medium-sized pan and put ground beef into it.

Cook until it becomes brown.

Add the onions along with bell peppers and sauté them with beef for 1-2 minutes.

Take a medium or large pot and combine onions, cooked meat, tomatoes, peppers, tomato paste, celery and water.

Sprinkle all the spices into the pot. Bring the ingredients to boil and then simmer on low heat for 1-2 hours. Stir every 30 minutes.

Serve hot.

Keto Quick Gravy

It takes hardly any time to prepare this gravy. It is very delicious for a complete meal at the breakfast table. The breakfast sausages absolutely complement the gravy. You can have this dish as a complete meal in itself or you can also have it as a side dish with burgers and salami sandwiches.

SERVES: 5

PREPARATION TIME: 10 min

INGREDIENTS:

Breakfast sausage	4 ounce
Butter	2 tablespoon
Heavy cream	1 cup

Guar gum powder	½
teaspoon	
Salt	as per taste
Pepper	as per taste
Cilantro	for garnishing

METHOD:

Take a large saucepan and heat it on medium-high heat.

Put the breakfast sausages in the pan and cook them until they become brown.

Take the sausages out with a deep spoon and leave the fat behind.

Put the butter into the pan and melt it.

Add heavy cream when the butter is melted. Stir when the bubbles are formed.

Put guar gum powder into the cream. Stir vigorously to burst the bubbles.

When the mixture becomes thick, you will notice that the gap left from stirring takes a while to fill in with gravy.

Put the sausages back into the pan and stir.

Serve hot.

Southern Spicy Chicken Salad

This is an amazingly simple chicken salad which uses up your leftover chicken and can be served with tomato wedges and pickles all piled onto a bed of lettuce for a quick fresh summer lunch.

SERVES: 5

PREPARATION TIME: 10 min

INGREDIENTS:

Cooked and chopped chicken
10-12 ounces

| Butter | 2 |

tablespoons

| Red onion (finely chopped) | 3 |

tablespoons

Celery (finely chopped)
  2-3 tablespoons

Chopped hard-boiled egg
  1 large

Dill pickle
  1 tablespoon

Mayonnaise
  ½ cup

Salt
  ¼ teaspoon

Black pepper (freshly ground)
  1/8 teaspoon

METHOD:

Take a medium sized sauté pan and heat it on medium high heat.

Melt the butter in the pan and put the chicken pieces into it.

Cook the chicken until it becomes brown.

Take it off the heat.

Take a medium-sized bowl and combine onions, chicken, eggs, and celery and toss them together.

Add the dill pickle, salt, mayonnaise, pepper and mix well.

Serve garnished with raw tomatoes and chopped mint leaves on a bed of lettuce.

Keto Spinach Soup

This soup is a superfood that you can never underestimate. All its ingredients are rich in nutrients. It gives you an ample supply of antioxidants, magnesium, potassium and lots of vitamins. It also gives you an ample amount of calcium without using any dairy products.

This will help kick off your "ketogeinc flu" which sometimes overcomes new followers of this diet.

SERVES:	5
PREPARATION TIME:	10 min
INGREDIENTS:	
Cauliflower (medium head)	1 or 400 grams

White onion (medium)	1
Garlic cloves	2
Crumbled bay leaf	1
Watercress	150 grams
Fresh spinach	200 grams
Vegetable or chicken stock	1 liter
Coconut milk or cream	1 cup
Coconut oil	¼ cup
Salt	1 teaspoon
Black pepper (freshly ground)	½ teaspoon
Chives/Parsley	for garnishing

METHOD:

Take a deep saucepan and put the coconut oil into it. When the oil is heated over medium heat, put in finely chopped garlic and onions. Sauté until the vegetables become tender.

Wash the watercress and spinach and keep aside.

Cut the florets of cauliflower and combine them with the onions.

Add the bay leaf and mix the ingredients well.

Add watercress and spinach leaves. Cook for 2-3 minutes until leaves are wilted.

Pour the in chicken or vegetable stock. Bring the mixture to a boil.

When the cauliflower becomes crisp-tender, pour in the coconut milk or cream.

Sprinkle with pepper and salt and mix well.

Take the saucepan off the heat and puree with a hand blender.

When the mixture is a nice creamy texture, it's ready to serve.

Pour some cream over the soup in the bowl just before serving.

Garnish with chives or parsley leaves.

Orange Coconut Drink

If you have to rush to the office on a Monday morning after a long weekend party, just wait for a second. Take just 10 minutes before you rush out and make this awesome and satisfying smoothie. It tastes amazing and will keep you energized for hours. Orange is not only good for your skin; it takes care of your heart as well.

SERVES: 4

PREPARATION TIME: 10 min

INGREDIENTS:

Orange juice	4 cups
Ice	2 cups
Coconut milk	1 can of ½ ounces
Honey	¼ cup
Shredded coconut	2 tablespoons
Orange slices	for garnish

METHOD:

Put the coconut milk, orange juice, honey and ice into a large jug and blend using a hand blender.

Puree until the mixture becomes very smooth.

You can also make it less smooth if you prefer a coarse texture.

Pour the smoothie into four glasses and garnish with orange slices and shredded coconut.

Salmon Spread

You can get as creative with serving this salmon spread as you want to be. Serve it as a dip or with a salad of tomatoes, cucumbers, bell peppers, etc. You can also use it as a filling for mushroom caps and serve it in a ready eat format at a get together.

It takes just 10 minutes to make then refrigerate it for an upcoming party.

SERVES: 5

PREPARATION TIME: 10 min

INGREDIENTS:

Cream cheese	12 ounces
Sour cream	1/3 cup
Lemon juice, fresh tablespoon	1
Tabasco sauce	6 dashes

Green and white parts of scallions	3
Drained and rinsed capers	3 tablespoons
Coarsely chopped smoked salmon	8 ounces
Fresh dill	3 tablespoons

METHOD:

Put sour cream, cream cheese, Tabasco and lemon juice in a food processor and pulse till they become a puree.

Add the capers, scallions, salmon, pepper and chopped dill. Blend them with the rest of the puree.

Take the puree out of the blender.

You can use this salmon spread with burgers, lettuce sandwiches, etc. You can also spread a mound of this salmon spread over chilled cucumber slices and serve it as a salad.

Fried Eggs With Cheddar Garlic and Cooking Grits

A quick recipe for a delicious breakfast. This will fill you up till lunchtime!

SERVES: 5

PREPARATION TIME: 10 min

INGREDIENTS:

Water	2 cups
Cooking grits	½ cup
Grated garlic clove	1
Cheddar cheese, grated	¼ cup
Chopped chives tablespoon	1
Large eggs	4
Salt and pepper taste	as per
Butter	½ teaspoon

METHOD:

Pour water into a small saucepan and bring it to boil.

When the water boils, reduce the heat to simmer or medium.

Put garlic and cooking grits in the pan and stir. Cover the pan with a lid.

Cook and stir frequently for 5-7 minutes until you find that the cooking grits are thickened.

Take the pan off the heat and add chives and grated cheddar cheese. Combine the ingredients well.

Add pepper and salt as per your taste. Keep the mixture aside.

Take a non-stick frying pan and heat it over medium heat.

Put some butter to grease the pan and crack the eggs in the frying pan. You can crack two eggs at a time.

Cook until the egg whites turn opaque.

Flip the eggs over and cook for a while.

Pour the cooking grits into shallow bowls and top with the eggs. Season with salt and pepper.

Serve immediately and piping hot.

Cup Omelets

Eggs are one thing which can be given any shape, size and look. You can add virtually anything to eggs and the outcome will be probably be good. Here, we have experimented to give eggs a new shape and added some vegetables. This is a perfect afternoon meal.

SERVES: 6

PREPARATION TIME: 10 min

BAKING TIME: 25 min

INGREDIENTS:

Eggs	4
Salt	as per taste
Pepper	as per taste
Diced bell pepper	½ cup
Diced tomato	½ cup
Diced cucumber	½ cup
Diced onions	½ cup
Shredded cheese	¾ cup
Chopped cilantro	for garnishing

METHOD:

Preheat the oven to at least 350 degrees.

Take a muffin pan with six cups and coat it with a cooking spray (nonstick).

Mix all the vegetables in a skillet and sauté them for 30 seconds.

Whisk all the eggs in a medium sized bowl.

Add diced vegetables to the bowl.

Add salt and pepper according to your taste.

Share out the mixture among the muffin cups and sprinkle shredded cheese over the top.

Put the muffin tray in the oven and bake for about 20-25 minutes. The edges of the omelets will become golden brown.

When you are about to remove the omelets from the cups, run a blunt butter knife around the cup edges to loosen.

Take out the omelet cups in a plate and garnish with a little cilantro.

Serve hot.

Tomato Scoops filled with Avocado

Little tomato halves stuffed with gorgeous creamy avocado. These make a delicious and colorful snack for any time of the day.

SERVES:	3-4
PREPARATION TIME:	15 min

INGREDIENTS:

Cherry tomatoes ounces	16
Mashed and peeled avocado	1 large
Lemon juice tablespoon	1
Onion (finely chopped)	1
Minced garlic	1 clove
Swiss cheese (finely shredded)	½ cup
Seasoning salt	¼ teaspoon

Bacon bits (bottled)   6 slices

METHOD:

Remove the top green part of the tomatoes. Cut about 1/3 part of the tomatoes.

Take a deep spoon and scoop out the seeds. Keep them for use in another dish. They will not be used in this recipe again.

Place the tomatoes on a paper towel with the cut-side facing downwards.

Cut the avocado and remove its pit.

Scoop out the flesh into a bowl and add seasoning salt and lemon juice.

Mash all the ingredients in the bowl using a fork. You can keep the mixture a little coarse.

Stuff the mixture of avocado into the tomato scoops.

Sprinkle some bacon bits on top and serve.

White Bean Salmon Salad

This delicious and filling salad makes a perfect light lunch or supper dish. The simple dressing compliments it perfectly, and as a bonus, the whole thing packs and keeps well in a lunchbox for work or school.

SERVES:	3-4
PREPARATION TIME:	15 min
INGREDIENTS FOR SALAD:	
Cannellini beans (15 ounces each)	2 cans
Pink salmon (3.75 ounces)	1 can
Parmesan cheese (freshly grated)	¼ cup
Red onion, minced	¼ cup
Minced garlic	1 clove
Tomatoes (cut into 8 pieces each)	2
Roughly chopped basil leaves	¼ cup

INGREDIENTS FOR DRESSING:

Vinegar tablespoons	3
Olive oil, extra virgin	¼ cup
Coarse salt teaspoon	¼
Ground pepper teaspoon	1/8

METHOD:

Remove beans from can, drain, and put them in a bowl.

Flake the salmon over the beans. Grate the parmesan cheese and sprinkle over the mixture.

Add the basil leaves, onions, tomatoes and minced garlic to the bowl.

Whisk the ingredients of the dressing together and pour it over the mixture of beans.

Gently toss the ingredients in the bowl and combine well.

Refrigerate the salad for 15 minutes and serve.

Chicken Lettuce Burrito

Do you miss your regular tortillas? Now you don't have to. The delicious lettuce rolls mentioned in the recipe will never let you say that you "can't eat those rolls anymore". You can have these lettuce rolls as much as you want without worrying about the side effects of wheat.

SERVES:
 3-4

PREPARATION TIME:
 15-20 min

INGREDIENTS:

Chicken breast (boneless halves)
    2 (skinless)

Tomato sauce   1
can (4 ounces)

Salsa
    ¼ cup

Diced bell peppers
    1

Chopped beans
    ½ cup

Taco seasoning mix
1.25 ounces

Ground cumin
    1 teaspoon

Minced garlic   2
cloves

Chili powder
    1 teaspoon

Hot sauce
    as per taste

Large lettuce leaves
8-10

METHOD:

Take a medium saucepan and heat it over medium heat.

Place tomato sauce and chicken breasts in the pan and cook until the sauce comes to boil.

Add salsa, cumin, garlic, chili powder and seasoning to the pan.

Simmer it for 15 minutes.

You can add a little water if you find that the mixture has become very thick.

Using 2 forks shred and pull the chicken meat off the main chunk into thin strings.

Add the bell peppers and beans to the pot.

Cook the strings and vegetables with lid on for another 8-10 minutes.

Add hot sauce as per your taste. Stir well.

When you find that the mixture has attained a thick consistency that can be easily wrapped, take it off the heat.

Place two layers of lettuce on a tray and fill it up with the filling.

Serve hot.

Shrimp Skewers and Lime Honey Dipping Sauce

Grilled shrimps are always good in summer. And what's better is when they are accompanied by a lime honey sauce. The freshness of the shrimps is retained even after cooking. They are just as good as they can get for a ketogenic diet. Indulge in this satisfying dish and enjoy the sunny day lunch.

SERVES:
>   3-4

PREPARATION TIME:
 15 min

INGREDIENTS (for shrimps):

Peeled shrimps
 1 pound

Salt
 1 teaspoon

Pepper
 ½ teaspoon

Garlic powder
 ½ teaspoon

Skewers
 3-4

INGREDIENTS (for lime honey sauce):

Olive oil
 1 tablespoon

Honey 3
full tablespoons

Limes for juice
  2 large

Lemon zest
  1 lemon

Chili powder
½ teaspoon

Cilantro
  ½ cup

METHOD (for shrimps):

Preheat a grill frying pan over a medium heat.

Spray the non-stick cooking spray around the pan.

Place the shrimps onto the skewers

Mix the pepper, salt and garlic powder and sprinkle the mixture over the shrimps.

METHOD (for sauce):

Take a small bowl and mix the honey, olive oil, chili powder, lime juice and lemon zest.

Take out 2 tablespoons of this mixture and brush the shrimps with it.

Keep the remaining sauce for serving.

After brushing the shrimps, grill them for 3-4 minutes.

After one side is cooked properly, flip them over and cook for 3-4 minutes.

When properly cooked the shrimps should look pinkish in color.

Take them off the heat. Place them in a plate and sprinkle some cilantro over them.

Serve with the lime honey sauce.

Zucchini Wraps

If you missed eating wraps in the ketogenic diet, here we are, with a beautiful option. These zucchini wraps are a completely healthy subsititute for those refined flour wraps.

They are spread with a fresh-tasting pesto, then layered with vegetable strips before being rolled up.

SERVES: 2

PREPARATION TIME:
15 min

INGREDIENTS (for wraps):

Thinly sliced zucchini (lengthwise)	3
Julienned bell pepper (red)	1
Julienned bell pepper (yellow)	1
Julienned quarters of carrots	1 carrot

Sprouts
    as per choice

Cilantro
    ¼ cup

Freshly ground black pepper   ¼ teaspoon

Toothpicks
7-8

INGREDIENTS (for kale pesto):

Basil leaves or kale	1 cup
Garlic	1 clove
Tahini	2 tablespoons
Olive oil, extra virgin	2 tablespoons
Himalayan salt	as per taste

METHOD:

For making the kale pesto, put the kale or basil leaves, garlic, tahini, olive oil and Himalayan salt into a food processor and pulse.

Add more seasoning if you feel it is needed.

Layer the zucchini slices on a chopping board. Layer on the pesto, bell peppers, carrots and sprouts. Roll the zucchini picking up the end where the vegetables are placed.

Stick the zucchini rolls with a toothpick in the middle. Sprinkle some freshly ground black pepper over the rolls.

Serve.

Eggs and Kale Blessing

Kale is a relatively new introduction to the American platter. But, it is the most nutrient dense vegetable of the cruciferous vegetable family. The high content of antioxidants in this leafy vegetable is not found anywhere else. Thus, it is ideal to include in a quick and healthy evening snack or an early morning breakfast.

SERVES: 1

PREPARATION TIME:
15 min

INGREDIENTS:

250

Butter	4 tablespoons	
Minced garlic	1 clove	
Kale	½ pound	
Eggs	2	
Coconut cream		1 tablespoon
Salt	1 pinch	
Freshly ground black pepper		¼ teaspoon

METHOD (for kale and eggs):

Take a small skillet and melt the butter in it over medium heat.

Add the minced garlic to the skillet. Cook it for a minute.

While the garlic cooks, trim the baby kale leaves from stems and wash them. Add them to the skillet.

Cover the skillet and let the baby kale cook for 5 minutes until wilted.

Remove from the skillet and keep warm.

Separate one of the eggs into yolk and white. Put in separate bowls.

Add one complete egg into the bowl containing only egg white.

Add one more tablespoon of butter into the skillet. Pour in the egg white mixture and cook until the egg white turns opaque.

METHOD (for sauce):

Microwave the coconut cream (1 tablespoon) and butter (2 tablespoons) just enough to melt them.

In the food processor, put a dash of salt, egg yolk (which we had separated earlier) and freshly ground black pepper.

Pulse the mixture and slowly pour the coconut cream and butter mix. Pulse the mixture till you have a smooth cream.

METHOD (for serving):

When ready to serve, place the kale in a plate. Place the fried egg over the kale. Spoon over as much sauce as you like.

Shrimp, Avocado and Spinach Salad with Lemon Zest Dressing

A lovely satisfying salad that serves as a light lunch or dinner. A bed of baby spinach topped with avocado, tomato and cucumber, shrimps, and dressed to perfection with a lemony dressing.

SERVES:
 3-4

PREPARATION TIME:
 15 min

INGREDIENTS:

Avocado	1
Baby spinach	5 ounces
Garlic	1 clove
Cherry tomatoes/ normal tomatoes	½ pint
Cucumber slices	8-10
Lemon juice	1 teaspoon

Lemon zest	½ lemon
Peeled shrimp	½ pound
Coconut oil	1 tablespoon

METHOD:

Wash the spinach and dry it on a paper towel.

Wash the cherry tomatoes and cut them into half. If you are using normal tomatoes, cut them into 8 wedges.

Halve the avocado and remove the pit. Scoop out the flesh with a melon baller.

Wash the shrimps under cold water and dry them on a paper towel.

Preheat a medium skillet.

Add the coconut oil to the skillet. Swirl the skillet so that the oil coats the bottom of the pan entirely.

Add garlic and let it cook until a gentle fragrance starts coming.

Add shrimps to the skillet and cook for 1-2 minutes on each side. The shrimps will become opaque when properly cooked.

To prepare the dressing, take a small bowl and put in the olive oil, lemon juice, lemon zest, honey, pepper and salt. Combine them together.

Arrange a layer of spinach on a plate. Put the avocado, tomatoes, cucumber slices and shrimps over the spinach. Pour some dressing and serve.

Flour Free Cheese Crackers

Sometimes, you just feel like munching something without any reason. For such cravings, we often resort to biscuits. Since it is better that you do not eat anything made of flour in the ketogenic diet; we have devised these cheese crackers for you. They will come in handy for those peckish moments when you want something crunchy to munch.

SERVES: 4

PREPARATION TIME:
 15 min

INGREDIENTS:

Cheese 8 ounces

Parchment paper
 for lining a baking dish

Seasoning
 ½ teaspoon

Mayonnaise
>   for serving

METHOD:

Preheat your oven to a temperature of 400 degrees.

Take a medium-sized baking sheet and line it with a parchment paper.

You can follow either one of two methods:

>   Shred cheese in a bowl and add some seasonings.
>   "or"

>   Cut the cheese into thin slices and sprinkle with seasoning.

Put tablespoons of shredded cheese onto the parchment. If you have cut slices (1/4 inch thickness) of cheese, place them on the parchment paper.

Leave a gap of 1 inch in between the cheese slices or piles.

Put the baking sheet into the oven and cook for 5-7 minutes.

You will notice that the edges of cheese will become brown when properly cooked.

Take out the baking dish and allow it to cool.

The cheese crackers will become crispy as they cool.

Serve them at room temperature later with mayonnaise or any other dip you like.

Bok Choy and Crispy Tofu Salad

This is a delicious recipe for tofu salad. The preparation does not take much time, but you do need to allow for some extra time for the marinating. Ultimately, the end result is of course worth it. You just need to plan ahead a little.

SERVES: 4

PREPARATION TIME:
25 min

MARINATING TIME:
5-6 hours

INGREDIENTS (tofu):

Firm tofu	15 ounces
Soy sauce	1 tablespoon
Sesame oil	1 tablespoon

Water	1 tablespoon
Minced garlic	2 teaspoons
Red wine vinegar	1 tablespoon
Lemon juice	1 teaspoon

INGREDIENTS (salad):

Bok choy	9 ounces
Green onion	2.5 ounces
Chopped cilantro	2 tablespoons
Coconut oil	3 tablespoons
Soy sauce	2 tablespoons
Sambal oelek (sauce)	1 tablespoon
Peanut butter	1 tablespoon
Lime juice	1 teaspoon
Liquid stevia	7 drops

METHOD:

Press the tofu dry for about 5-6 hours before cooking.

To prepare the marinade, combine the soy sauce, water, sesame oil, lemon juice, vinegar and garlic.

Make small dices of tofu and marinate them in the mixture for at least 30 minutes. It is better if you leave it to marinate for 5-6 hours.

Preheat your oven to 350 degrees.

Take a medium-sized baking sheet and line it with parchment paper.

Place the marinated tofu onto the baking sheet and cook for 30-35 minutes.

While the tofu is baking, take a bowl and combine all the ingredients for the salad dressing, leaving the bok choy aside.

Chop the bok choy into small pieces.

Remove the tofu from the oven.

Arrange the tofu, bok choy and salad dressing on a plate and serve.

Zucchini Pasta and Basil-Cashew Pesto

Did you think that you would not be able to have all those delicious pastas when you're are on a keto diet? Well, it is better that you say goodbye to those unhealthy refined flour pastas. We have a much healthier option for you. It's zucchini pasta! The pesto sauce along with this green vegetable is so tasty.

SERVES: 2

PREPARATION TIME:
　　15 min

INGREDIENTS:

Basil leaves	½ cup
Minced garlic	2 cloves
Cashew nuts (raw)	¼ cup
Olive oil (extra virgin)	¼ cup
Lime juice	1 tablespoons

Nutritional yeast	1.5 tablespoons
Zucchini	2
Salt	½ teaspoon

METHOD:

Put the basil leaves, garlic, cashew nuts, olive oil, lime juice and yeast in a food processor and pulse to make the pesto.

Using a spiralizer, make noodles out of the zucchini.

Take a skillet and sauté zucchini pasta.

Remove the pasta from the skillet and put it into a bowl.

Remove the pesto from the food processor and mix it with the pasta.

Serve with a smile.

Cheese Broccoli Soup

SERVES: 2

PREPARATION TIME: 15 min

INGREDIENTS:

Pastured butter	2 tablespoons
Chicken broth	3 cups
Organic cream cheese	8 ounces
Heavy cream	1 cup
Cheddar cheese, shredded	2 cups
Chopped fresh broccoli bunches	2

METHOD:

Take a deep saucepan and put the chicken broth and broccoli into it.

Bring to the boil and cook until the broccoli becomes tender.

Take a frying pan and put it on the heat.

Put in the heavy cream, shredded cheese, cream cheese, and butter. Stir well.

Take half of the broccoli from the pot and puree it in a food processor.

Pour the melted mixture from the pan into the saucepan of broth. Put the pureed broccoli from the food processor into the broth as well.

Combine well. Add pepper and salt according to taste.

When you feel that the soup has reached a desired thickness and is a good consistency, ladle into soup bowls.

Garnish with cheese.

Serve hot.

Avocado Wrapped in Bacon

Creamy avocado with salty bacon! Sounds delicious doesn't it? These bites of bacon wrapped avocadoes are just perfect when you are on the go. You can grab these bits of health while you are still packing your bag for the office. Or there are times when you are getting ready at 6 pm for a dinner party. You feel hungry but you do not want to overeat before dinner. These bacon wraps come in handy at such rush hours.

SERVES: 2

PREPARATION TIME:
   15 min

INGREDIENTS:

Chili powder	1 teaspoon
Brown sugar	¼ cup
Avocado	1
Bacon	4-6 slices

METHOD:

Preheat your oven to 425 degrees.

Take a medium sized baking dish and line it with foil.

Take a small bowl and mix the brown sugar and chili powder.

Cut the avocado in half and remove its pit. Cut thin slices of avocado about ¾ inches thick.

Cut the slices of bacon into 3-5 pieces.

Wrap the bacon slices around the pieces of avocado.

Roll the wraps in the mixture of brown sugar and chili.

Place the rolls on the baking tray.

Cook for 10-15 minutes.

Take out the wraps on a plate and stick a toothpick in the center.

Serve.

Salmon Baked with Herbs

The herb fragrance while the salmon is baking is sure to get your mouth watering! This makes a lovely light dinner dish. As a bonus, the dish is completed with minimum hassle. If salmon is eaten regularly, it prevents depression and lethargic thinking, and is good for eye health too. Moreover, if you are suffer from insomnia, it will help you have a good sleep. Salmon is called a "happy food" because of the many health benefits it offers.

SERVES: 2

PREPARATION TIME:
30-40 min

INGREDIENTS:

Salmon fillet with skin	12 ounces
Finely chopped shallot	1
Chopped parsley	2 tablespoons
Chopped basil	2 tablespoons
Dried / fresh dill	1 tablespoon
Lemon zest, finely grated tablespoon	1
Olive oil	1 tablespoon
Sea salt	½ teaspoon

METHOD:

An hour prior to your beginning this recipe, you need to do this preparation:

Remove salmon from your refrigerator and let it come to room temperature.

Take a pan and fill it half with water. Place it on the lower rack of the oven; preheat the oven at a temperature of 250 degrees.

METHOD (to make the herb paste)

Chop the parsley, shallot, and basil with other herbs. Mix the lemon zest and olive oil into this mixture.

Grease a rack with oil and place it over the baking tray.

Position the fillet of salmon on the rack with the skin side facing downwards.

Coat the top side of the salmon with a thick layer of the herb mixture. You can coat the sides too if the herb paste does not fall off.

Put the salmon in the middle rack of the oven. Bake it for 25-30 minutes.

If your fillet is quite thick, it might require more time.

Take out the salmon and close the door.

Insert a knife in the thickest portion of salmon and check whether it is cooked. If it flakes easily, it is ready. If not, put it back into the oven for further baking. Check again after 5 more minutes.

Take out the salmon and cut it into 2-3 pieces. Remove the skin with the help of a spatula.

Sprinkle with salt and serve.

Peppermint Bombs

Chocolate and mint are a brilliant combination, and a perfect ending to a lovely meal.

SERVES: 2

PREPARATION TIME:
15-20 min

INGREDIENTS:

Coconut butter	¾ cup
Shredded coconut	1/3 cup

Coconut oil	3 tablespoons
Peppermint extract	½ teaspoon
Cocoa powder	2 tablespoons

METHOD:

Combine the coconut butter (melted), shredded coconut, coconut oil (1 tbsp) and peppermint extract.

Stir well and pour the mixture into small sweet moulds. Fill the moulds only half way.

Place the moulds in the refrigerator for 15 minutes.

Mix the coconut oil (2 tbsp) and cocoa powder in a bowl.

Take out the moulds from the refrigerator. Pour the cacao mixture into the moulds over the peppermint.

Put the moulds back in the refrigerator.

When the bombs harden, take them out of the fridge 5 minutes before serving.

Pistachio Almond Fat Bombs

Almonds and pistachios are always a treat. Put them in anything and you can transform even the most boring dish in the world. Your family is bound to love these little morsels. Keep them a secret and surprise your family after dinner. Nobody will be able to resist them.

SERVES: 2

PREPARATION TIME:
   15 min

INGREDIENTS:

Cocoa butter	½ cup
Almond butter	1 cup
Coconut butter, creamy	1 cup
Coconut oil	1 cup
Coconut milk, full fat	½ cup
Ghee/ clarified butter	¼ cup
Vanilla extract	1 tablespoon
Salt	¼ teaspoon
Chai spice	2 teaspoons

METHOD:

Take a baking dish and line it with parchment paper. Leave a little paper hanging on both sides. It will help you to unmold it easily.

Take a saucepan and melt the cocoa butter over low heat.

Take a bowl and mix the almond butter, coconut butter, firm oil of coconut, coconut milk, clarified butter, vanilla extract, chai spice, almond extract and salt. Blend the ingredients well.

Pour the cocoa butter from the pan into the mixture and combine well.

Transfer the mixture into baking dish and spread it evenly.

Sprinkle with chopped pistachios (raw).

Keep it in the fridge for 4 hours or overnight.

Take the pan out next day and cut it into small pieces.

Serve chilled.

Mushroom Sauce and Steak

Mushrooms along with steak is just an awesome combination. Try this recipe and you will fall in love with it.

SERVES: 2

PREPARATION TIME:
 15 min

INGREDIENTS:

Rib eye steak	2 pounds
Salt	1 teaspoon
Pepper	¼ teaspoon
Butter	1 tablespoon
Port wine	4 ounces
Sliced Mushrooms	10 ounces
Heavy cream	2 ounce

METHOD:

Preheat your oven to 450 degrees Fahrenheit.

Sprinkle the pepper and salt on both sides of steak.

Take a cast iron skillet and heat it on high.

Put in butter and let it bubble.

Put steak in butter and cook it for 2 minutes on each side.

Take out the steak and put it in the oven.

Bake the steak in the oven until the desired internal temperature of the steak is reached. It should be 135 degrees for rare.

Take the steak out and cover it with a foil.

Add port wine to the skillet to deglaze. Scrape off all the tasty bits that are stuck on the skillet.

Add mushrooms and heavy cream.

Let the sauce simmer and thicken.

Pour the sauce over the cooked steak.

Serve hot.

Conclusion

After reading so many recipes based on the ketogenic diet, you must be feeling relaxed that you do not have to give up on your favorite foods that contain fat. You can freely eat whatever meat you want. Moreover, there is a wide range of options available for vegans as well. You do not have to give up on your favorite dishes.

The best part of the ketogenic diet is that you can eat meats, cheese, mayonnaise, etc. and just cut down a little on the carbohydrates. The body gradually adapts to utilize fats for energy instead of carbohydrates. It means that you do not have to make any extra effort to shed off the extra fat on your body. Your body will automatically make that effort for you. Carbohydrates make you feel sleepy for hours but fats don't.

When you are on a high carbohydrate diet, the body anticipates high energy sources to keep coming to it. But when you are on a high fat and low carbohydrate diet, your body has to organize itself to mobilize the fats it receives as an energy source.

A very important benefit of this diet is that fats keep you feeling satiated for longer. It means that you eat a lot of fats but actually you do not have to eat all day to satisfy your hunger. But, carbohydrates make you feel hungry again and again. The volume of your food decreases but the amount of calories taken in by your body remains adequate.

Adapting to a ketogenic diet takes at least 2-3 weeks depending upon the person. So please be patient when you start this new lifestyle for yourself.

Disclaimer:

The information presented in this book represents the views of the publisher as of the date of publication. The publisher reserves the rights to alter update their opinions based on new conditions. This report is for informational purposes only. The author and the publisher do

not accept any responsibilities for any liabilities resulting from the use of this information. While every attempt has been made to verify the information provided here, the author and the publisher cannot assume any responsibility for errors, inaccuracies or omissions. Any similarities with people or facts are unintentional.

www.ingramcontent.com/pod-product-compliance
Lightning Source LLC
LaVergne TN
LVHW010312070526
838199LV00065B/5530